A Man of Utterance

Also by Ian Brinton:

Dickens's "Great Expectations" (Reader's Guides)
       (London: Continuum, 2007)

Contemporary Poetry: Poets and Poetry since 1990
       (Cambridge Contexts in Literature; Cambridge: Cambridge
       University Press, 2009)

A Manner of Utterance

The Poetry of J.H. Prynne

edited by

Ian Brinton

To Paul,
with all best
wishes.

August 11.

Shearsman Books
Exeter

Published in the United Kingdom in 2009 by
Shearsman Books Ltd
58 Velwell Road,
Exeter EX4 4LD

ISBN 978-1-84861-042-2 (Hardcover)
ISBN 978-1-84861-043-9 (Paperback)
First Edition

Acknowledgements
An earlier version of the essay by Richard Humphreys, and its
accompanying interview with Ian Friend, was published in *On Paper*
(Brisbane: Andrew Baker, 2008). An earlier version of Keston Sutherland's
essay previously appeared in *British Poetry 1945–2007*, eds. Robin Purves
and Sam Ladkin (Prague: Litteraria Pragensia, 2007). Simon Perril's essay
previously appeared in *Jacket* (2002). Ian Brinton's essay first appeared in
PN Review 171 (2006).
All quotations from the poetry of J.H. Prynne are drawn from *Poems*
(Bloodaxe Books / Fremantle Arts Centre Press, 2005), are copyright ©
J.H. Prynne, and are reproduced here by kind permission of the author.
Quotations from other works by J.H. Prynne are likewise copyright ©
J.H. Prynne and are reproduced here with the author's permission. The
quote from Tom Raworth on page 15 is copyright © Tom Raworth and is
reproduced with his permission. The poem 'The Land Below" by Edward
Dorn, collected in Edward Dorn *Collected Poems* (revised edition, Four
Seasons Press, San Francisco, 1984) is copyright © Edward Dorn, 1964, and
is excerpted here by kind permission of Jennifer Dunbar, on behalf of the
author's estate.

Cover: detail from *Star Damage at Home #2* (2007–2008), Indian ink,
gouache and pen on khadi paper; 23 x 30 cm, by Ian Friend. Copyright ©
Ian Friend, 2008. Reproduced by permission of the artist.

CONTENTS

INTRODUCTION

Ian Brinton

How the poets were the first philosophers, the first astronomers and historiographers and orators and musicians of the world

Utterance also and language is given by nature to man for persuasion of others and aid of themselves—I mean the first ability to speak. For speech itself is artificial and made by man, and the more pleasing it is the more it prevaileth to such purpose as it is intended for; but speech by metre is a kind of utterance more cleanly couched and more delicate to the ear than prose is, because it is more current and slipper upon the tongue, and withal tuneable and melodious, as a kind of music, and therefore may be termed a musical speech or utterance, which cannot but please the hearer very well. Another cause is for that it is briefer and more compendious, and easier to bear away and be retained in memory, than that which is contained in multitude of words, and full of tedious ambage and long periods. It is, beside, a manner of utterance more eloquent and rhetorical than the ordinary prose which we use in our daily talk, because it is decked and set out with all manner of fresh colours and figures, which maketh that it sooner inveigleth the judgement of man, and carrieth his opinion this way and that, whither soever the heart, by impression of the ear, shall be most affectionately bent and directed.

George Puttenham, *The Art of English Poesy*, 1589.

This collection of essays by musicians, visual artists, academics and teachers revolves around the notion of what is involved in the activity of reading and, in particular, what effect the reading of the poetry of J.H. Prynne has had upon them. It is not a Reader's Guide; it does not provide answers. Instead it offers personal and deeply felt reactions to reading Prynne's poetry and discovering what Douglas Templeton refers to when he says that for him the poems "put ambiguity in the foreground" where they "achieve an authenticity by acknowledging the dangerous spaces in language."

The book's genesis lay partly in my trying to reconcile within myself the views of two readers whose attitudes towards Prynne's poetry seemed so widely divergent, ranging from the quietly serious to the ludicrous. Randall Stevenson's suggestion in volume 12 of *The*

Oxford English Literary History that Prynne's "full significance for the period's poetry began to be realised only at the end of the century" seemed wildly at odds with Don Paterson's comment in an article published in November 2004 in *The Guardian* ('Rhyme and reason'). In the latter it is suggested that readers find whatever they want in their reading: "The Norwich phone book or a set of log tables would serve them as well as their Prynne, in whom they seem able to detect as many shades of mind-blowing confusion as Buddhists do the absolute." The former appears in an academic book which goes some way in charting the literary developments taking place in England between 1960 and 2000, the latter in a daily newspaper; what they share in common is that both say something about the art of reading.

The sense of relationship between the poet and the reader has been intriguingly highlighted in the recently published book by Dr. Li Zhi-min, *New Chinese Poetry under the Influence of Western Poetics: The Origins, Development and Sense of Nativeness*:

> In the face of difficult poetry, there certainly should be a change of attitude towards 'understanding' itself, so that one can feel confident to understand an 'obscure' poem in an 'obscure' way.

In terms of reading being a lifelong occupation, Li Zhi-min also brings to our attention an attitude of traditional Chinese reading:

> Traditionally, Chinese readers often read a good poem again and again, in a loud voice and by murmuring, in imagination and in meditation; in doing so they naturally enjoy the poetical beauties. And sometimes in China one may often memorise a poem one does not understand; only dozens of months or even dozens of years later to experience a sudden enlightenment and full enjoyment of the poem. Poetry is written to be read, not to be analysed.

Prynne himself has said quite a bit about reading, from the generous review of Chris Torrance's 1968 book of poems, *Green Orange Purple*

Red (*Grosseteste Review* Autumn 1969) to the more recent 'Tips on Practical Criticism for Students of English' and its companion piece, 'Tips on Reading', January 2004. In the former he praises Torrance's "singing voice of such persuasive and dilated movement" which "has not for a long time been heard in the land", words which might well be attributed to his own singing grace. In reference to 'Practical Criticism', a term to describe a Cambridge invention introduced by I.A. Richards in the 1920s, he suggests that "Regular exercises in close reading both sharpen and deepen accurate response to local texture and also feed into enhanced perception of larger-scale structure, to make us all-round better readers."

Those comments made by Li Zhi-min about traditional Chinese reading suggest a significant amount of trust and willing engagement on the part of the reader and if this were to prompt the question as to what one might read in this trusting way then perhaps we should also note Douglas Templeton's reaction to his reading of Prynne:

> There is something about the voice of these poems which led me to trust the author.

Also referring to that engagement between text and reader, reviewing *Unanswering Rational Shore* (*Poetry Review* Vol. 92, No. 2, Summer 2002) Jeremy Noel-Tod suggested that Prynne's poetry "will be misunderstood if it is looked at, and not read" and this echoes Veronica Forrest-Thomson's recognition that Prynne's poetry sought to "make language real again for the poet and the reader" (*Poetic Artifice*, Manchester University Press, 1978).

In that *Grosseteste* review of nearly forty years ago, Prynne referred to Torrance's singing voice as being "covert, aware of distance held off by a species of pearly haze, small faces of the actual suddenly but without surprise revealing an intimate curve." In an echoing image which appears in *The First Students' English Magazine* printed at Guangzhou University in May 2005, suggesting a fine sense of continuity which is certainly not to be confused with repetition, he recognised the 'brilliant' quality of the new magazine which had arisen from the reading involved in the Guangzhou University English Writing Classes "full of pearl-bright moments and shining articles all moving along in the currents of these changing times."

Perhaps the last word here ought to be given to Jeremy Prynne as a teacher as well as a poet. In his extensive notes of advice, those 'Tips' given to students of English, he highlights the central importance of reading in relation to humanity and, in a way, prepares us for the reactions of those contributors whose engagement with the lifetime's work of this central figure has proved to be the real starting-point for this book:

> When a reading of text has proceeded by laborious stages within the test-rig of detailed study, pause to allow the overall effect to integrate back into a coherent human reading, and ponder whether your life may even have been changed, just a little, or your beliefs about large questions; whether your habits of feeling have been flattered or boastfully challenged, or whether your relation to the text builds up a kind of trust. This aspect is what you will take away with you when all the study is finished, and it should last you through a lifetime.

'HIS BRILLIANT LUMINOUS SHADE'

Ian Brinton

Edward Dorn's long poem, 'The Land Below', was first printed under the title 'The Landscapes Below' in *The Floating Bear 3*, 1961, before being extensively revised for inclusion in issue six of the Cambridge journal, *Prospect*, edited in 1964 by Jeremy Prynne. *The Floating Bear*, edited by LeRoi Jones and Diane di Prima, was a mimeographed newsletter which was distributed through the Phoenix Bookstore, New York, and was offered to the reader free of charge, or for the price of paper and postage. This dislocation from the market forces was mirrored in the information at the end of *Prospect* 6: 'Only a very small number of copies will be for sale over a counter; but copies will be sent free of charge to any person, who, out of a real sense of interest, thinks it worth writing to the editor to ask for them.' 'The Land Below' also appeared in Dorn's second published volume of poems, *Hands Up!* (Totem Press/LeRoi Jones) in 1964, the year before the young American was awarded a Fulbright Lectureship at the newly-founded University of Essex.

Dorn's poem opens with a delicate sense of exactness:

> The light wind falters leaves
> in the cottonwood. Barely evening.
> The rain earlier, coming again
> from the West, in front of me.

> Over the Jemez an illumined band of milk grey
> where the afterglow lingers.   Nearer,
> in front, a tower
> two red lights come on and off.
> A set for the evening.

The relationship between time and place is then conveyed in a juxtaposition between Colorado and New Mexico and from there with Homeric Troy:

> Below the sky
> the breeze is mingled with rain in New Mexico

a small sound and an earlier evening
than in Colorado, the tiers of my country
are ascending shades, but in the descending sunlight
evening comes and comes.

As upon

another day, before evening,
a darker one
on what kind of day,
did beautiful Hector rise
from his bed and smile,
the day his death beckoned was
it steel grey iron, and does the sun
shine early on Asia Minor?

With the inevitability of falling night's arrival and in association with
the tiers or levels of both history and geography we have been taken
back to the world of Troy and the death of Hector. The two joining
words, 'As upon', held with their double line-spacing both before and
after, perhaps convey a distance which is also at the same time being
conflated. With his mind not upon the fragments of archaeological
discovery made by Schliemann whose nineteenth-century excavations
claimed to have unearthed the original site of Troy, Dorn's concern is
for the common links between the past and the present:

Do the leaves fly up in the wind
at eight o'clock along the shadows
of those hills?   this is all I care about
those commons.

Dorn enquires not after the great Hector but after the armour-bearer,
the common man, the most direct connecting link between the past
and the present:

Whose arm carried his armour, I asked
myself, what

must he have been like, looked
downtrodden probably, as one
today, going into battle against
all those big greezers.
And there goes Hector to work
across the plain of olives
                    I wonder
if it had come noon yet, Achilles
(mere discus thrower) killed that man
there on the coast, shame, Schliemann
did you find your pots and sherds?

But what happened to that man the arms bearer?
I still wonder what happened to that caddy.
Take your pots and sites . . .

The common link between the past and the present is emphasised next
by an association between the 'caddy' for Hector and 'Ford workers/
or generations of workers father & son'. Both are downtrodden by
going into battle against 'all those big greezers' who are themselves
defined by the most simple of economic theories:

(They simply get
what they want—
an economy is *never*
more intricate
than that

Those 'pots and sherds' which the archaeologist collects do not
bring back the reality of a past; they merely allow a peeking into 'the
backyard/ of our eternity':

Fossils look
a great deal alike, taken in haste
from the great ranges, are more or less
undistinguishable in the sub-terra ranges
and mines earth-long and imponderably heavy.

13

The connecting link is how much does not change despite the advertisers of modernity selling progress:

> Yes,
> any kind of house
> will stand.   Principles are very misleading.
> Once you have found one or two
> you can build a library let alone a house.
> Take 1931–1941 as a decade.   It is funny now,
> so effete. When you see one of those old
> people riding a horse with a red saddle
> through the streets shouting "Times change"—
> What a lie.   They do not change.   Or,
> have not.

Dorn's interest in 'the backyard of our eternity' is recorded by his biographer, Tom Clark, who recalled a journey they both made in 1979 across the upper Plains following the Belle Fourche up towards the Badlands. Clark recalls 'looking out over two hundred miles of prairie' and seeing nothing, looking 'at the horizon rim the sky trembled and shone, in between the space looked completely empty':

> Ed then filled it in with the substantial history of everything
> that had happened out there going back beyond the Plains
> Indians to the movements of the earth-plates and the ice. He
> was always giving you everything—the most generous man it
> was possible to know.
> (*A World of Difference*, North Atlantic Books 2002)

This practice of reading the landscape was something which Dorn had taken from Charles Olson who had mentioned, in his 1955 'Bibliography of America for Edward Dorn', the importance of the geographer Carl Sauer and had given him a copy of Sauer's 1925 University of California publication, *The Morphology of Landscape*. Tom Clark referred to Dorn's reading of Sauer:

> Looking at the land with an eye trained by an Olson or a
> Sauer, Dorn learned to see its crucial role in determining

cultural and individual fates; how, say, in Olson's paraphrase of Sauer, a 'prairie village called Chicago is still, despite itself, a prairie village.'

Or, as Jeremy Prynne wrote in one of the 1968 *Kitchen Poems*, 'A Gold Ring Called Reluctance', reprinted in the 2005 volume *Poems* (Bloodaxe/Fremantle Arts Centre Press):

> Even the most
> modern shops, if you work at them, will
> resolve into streets or thoroughfares; their
> potential for transfer has simply been absorbed,
> by trade.

Tom Raworth had written to Dorn in April 1961 about what he saw as the moribund state of poetry in England at the time:

> It's odd—poetry over here is, I think, still a 'class' thing—don't know why. There's no flow: no use of sort of natural language. The whole thing is so artificial & contrived. I mean you read the stuff and it's just *reading*. Does absolutely nothing. Feel that they've sat down with a bag of assorted 'poetical' words and arranged them: and that's all. Nothing has the power to MOVE.

The poetry of Edward Dorn is all about movement both historical and geographical, seeing oneself in terms of time and place; awareness of movement requires more than a collection of Schliemann's 'pots and sherds'. When Prynne lent his copy of Dorn's first volume, *The Newly Fallen* (Totem Press 1961) to Donald Davie he was able to write to the American poet in the following terms:

> I recently lent Donald Davie my copy of 'The Newly Fallen' and he wrote to me 'I don't know when I enjoyed reading a collection of poems so much as Edw. Dorn's'—this is an encouraging comment from an academic of such intelligence & standing as he is, and I mean encouraging for us, in that this narrow and opinionated world here is perhaps now beginning

to open up and admit the importance of a modern American writing.

In 1961, Vista had published a *Beat Poets* addition to its Pocket Poets series which included Dorn as well as Corso, Ferlinghetti, Ginsberg and Snyder amongst eight others. Prynne's reaction to the little publication was recorded in the same letter:

> I saw the Vista anthology, and could feel the coy patronage which its issue here reflects; the idea being, I take it, that after the most vigorous winnowing, beat poetry can be scaled down to the manageable drawing-room level that enjoy curiosities of that kind.

Open Field composition was an attempt to keep alive a continuous exchange of energy: 'the full circuit of object, image, action'. Olson's contemporary reality is not on 'the manageable drawing-room level' but involves a rather larger area: 'At root (or stump) what *is*, is no longer THINGS but what happens BETWEEN things, these are the terms of the reality contemporary to us—and the terms of what we are.' ('The Escaped Cock', 1951). This not only brings to mind the necessary engagement between text and reader, world and viewer, but also a care for the lost ordinariness of moments of which life is constituted. What *did* happen to Hector's armour-bearer? Or, as Prynne puts it in 'A Gold Ring Called Reluctance':

> And so slowness is
> interesting and the dust, in cracks between
> boards. The old ones have their senses
> in the elegant droop they sometimes con-
> trive, the knowing falter that makes it
> all like some trick. Fluff, grit, various
> discarded bits & pieces: these are the
> genetic patrons of our so-called condition.

In the last section of Dorn's poem he accompanies his family on a Fourth of July picnic celebration which involves a journey in time as well as space:

As we came down
             into the green pines
the sharp brushes raking our faces
greeted by cooler air,
the children ran on
             looking
for a table.
Walking on the path
I saw alders again.   Very good.
We were on the revolutionary earth—

As they sit down they see an Indian at another table:

He wore a green shirt, otherwise
he retained a solitude, his lean ankles crossed.
And the hair done up in back
with a simple white tight wound cloth
and girding his hair and forehead
a patterned handkerchief, a forelock hanging
over, the longer hair bobbed around his head.

Dorn borrows a light from their fire and stands on the edge of this group, smoking while the women joke pleasantly, laughing

             it would
cost a dime for the light, it was going
to rain, they had just performed a dance,
they might even scalp us (noticing the
whiteness of the children's hair). But the Old Man
hardly smiled, at least one couldn't tell,
the grimness of his lips, I felt my scalp tingle,
did it engage his memory?

But having had a light from an ember
and standing there, I marvelled at the beauty
of men who have long hair.   Yes, it is quite
different.   Their world.   I am sure they tread

upon an Earth I don't. And I would like to.
Not facilely, or for long, but to be with them
for a spell, the chatter
of the women really distraction, everything
they had, gone up in smoke.   It must have been their idea
to camp, imagine, Indians camping.

Playing Indian. They take too lightly
their breed, forcing me to take too lightly
what I am.   But ah,
the man is so old, has emphatically not
made the change as they
in their tapered pants.

This moment of recognition on Dorn's part is not the same as Schliemann's collection of 'pots and sherds', it is not a piecing together of a past from fragments, but is closer to what Prynne calls 'inhabiting the moment rather than any restriction of awareness.' ('Tomorrow is Fade Out Night', a review published in *Prospect 6* of Douglas Woolf's novel, *Fade Out*).

But Beauty is remarkable in that you
can never return to it.   It never
exists again, once having been there.
And this instant I relate; this long
haired, slow to look creature, sitting once again
ankles crossed at a bench—only their heads remain,
from the gullet down, that dull gondola,
the automatic body, is just like ours
would you believe it, scoffing wieners
and 7 up.

Fade Out, Douglas Woolf's second novel, had been published by Grove Press in 1959 and it depicted the journey taken by two retired old men who escape the stifling, emasculating and bullying concern of their families to settle for a different quality of living in a near-abandoned ghost town. Prynne's respect for this prose is evident from his *Prospect* review which was published in the same issue as Dorn's poem:

> The real interest, and honesty, of this tale lie in the rhythm
> which defines the narrative's continuity. For the earlier life in
> New York is depicted in great density of detail, which clogs
> it and weighs it down to a standstill. The westward journey is
> the great illusion, whereby the rhythms of living may expand
> into a more fluid measure; but this has been more often theme
> than experience . . .
>   FADE OUT shows how as the choice is made for a more
> fluent way of living the density of a static environment does
> actually thin out, so that the curve flattens into a great arc at
> least reaching for the Pacific. It is important that Twombley
> doesn't wish to reach the coast. He has no urgent concern
> to arrive, but simply to suspend the urgency of that sort of
> concern. Nearly two-thirds of the narrative is held down
> within the city limits of New York, and yet the novel is
> essentially trajectory, the Homeric passage into the warmth
> of a New Greece.

Prynne notes what he calls 'this thinning line' of narrative as the two
wanderers approach the point where it will be possible to rest:

> The incidents become almost comatose, with a confidence of
> inhabiting the moment rather than any restriction of awareness.
> There is just progressively less to be said. The encounters
> become more random, less connected, more complete facts.
> Persons take on a kind of luminous containment, which
> again these two can deal with by being old: they have enough
> coloured slides to last what remains of a life-time. The way
> Woolf drains the last ripple of urgency out of the movement
> without diminishing the presence of these two men and the
> landscape is very lovely, so that when they come to a total halt
> in a near-abandoned ghost town, just short of their avowed
> destination, the discrepancies of all the earlier irony have been
> accounted for, displaced in the rarification of the transit. The
> ground is green and tawny by turns, and the openness to

what is humanly seen and felt becomes purged of intention.
A chastity of knowledge overtakes them, and they disappear
into a hotel under the sea.

This thinning-out of density, an awareness of the clutter which lies
in the 'backyard/of our eternity', is central to Prynne's poem 'In the
Long Run, to be Stranded' (published in *The White Stones*, 1969, *Poems*
p.47):

> Finally it's trade that the deep changes
> work with, so that the lives are heavier,
> less to be moved from or blunted. The city
> is the language of transfer
> > to the human account. Here
> > the phrases shift, the years
> > are an acquiescence.

The connection between movement (tread) and the exchange of
commodities associated with 'trade' is held in the word's derivation: a
path, course of action, borrowed from Middle Dutch or Middle Low
German *trade*, track; Old Saxon *trada*, footstep.

> > This isn't a wild comment: there's no
> good in the brittle effort, to snap the pace
> into some more sudden glitter of light:
> > hold to this city or the slightly pale
> > walking, to a set rhythm of
> > the very slight hopefulness. That
> is less than patience, it's time or more clearly
> the sequence of years; a thickening in the words
> as the coins themselves wear thin and could
> > almost balance on the quick
> > ideal edge.

The irony of more being less, the accumulation of those objects
bought by trade and the filling out of language that almost clogs the
tongue is not to be angrily repudiated. There is a quietness of tone
here which seems to settle for lowered sights:

> The stirring is so
> slight, the talk so stunned, the
> city warm in the air, it is a
> too steady shift, and life as
> it's called is age and the merest impulse,
> called the city and the deep
> blunting damage of hope.
> That's where it is, now
> as the place to be left and the last
> change still in return: down there
> in the snow, too, the loyal city of man.

Just as Prynne plays with the multiple meanings of 'trade' and 'change' (what one gets in return during the transaction) so he also holds the reader in a tension between two opposite meanings of 'stranded': the shore or beach may be where we find ourselves 'in the long run' but the individual fibres of a rope are both broken and formed in the verb 'to strand'.

The poetry of both Dorn and Prynne shares a concern with how the land has developed in relation to trade and one of the central influences here again is Carl Sauer. In 'Homestead and Community on the Middle Border' (*Landscape, Vol. 12, No. 1* 1962), Sauer looks at the effects of the 1862 Homestead Act in terms of the westward movement of families seeking land to cultivate and to own. The area he dealt with was Dorn's own family and social background which had been recorded in 'On the Debt My Mother Owed to Sears Roebuck', also printed in *Prospect 6*, as the world of trade is inextricably bound up with day-to-day existence:

> ... man's ways winged their way to her through the mail
> saying so much per month
> so many months, this is yours, take it
> take it, take it, take it

In 1966, Dorn published his book, *The Shoshoneans*, a text accompanied by the photographs of Leroy Lucas (William Morrow and Company, New York). Near the beginning he records a visit he made to the 102 year-old Shoshoni, Willie Dorsey:

The volume of his voice, the force of his gesture, were low keyed but so articulate and registered I could hardly make the adjustment, no matter how I intended to know, to align with his sense. His engagement with the room and all in it was pure. Life for him had turned into full rite, the tone of his existence was self-measuring. The act of his presence was a total rhythmic manifestation from his gesture to the inward mirror of his eyes. He barely moved, only his lips were the agents of the muscles of his neck and eyes, the ends of a network of force around his head. His English seemed fair, the problem was his hearing, I thought.

J.H. Prynne's recently published *Poems* is dedicated to Edward Dorn, 'his brilliant luminous shade' and Dorn's copy of 'The Morphology of Landscape' which Olson had given him now rests in the library of the English poet.

Notes Towards a Preliminary Reading of J.H. Prynne's *Poems*

David Caddy

The arc of J.H. Prynne's poetry over the past forty years may be said to have broadly moved from a metaphorically based open field lyricism towards a metonymic and etymological challenge to the reader. It is, above all, concerned with encouraging the reader on a journey, involving a reading process that avoids closure. It is about the journey, that is a continual process, towards meaning and comprehension rather than finding answers. It places utterance within the political and socio-economic predicament of the individual in relation to its historical and geographical landscape. One might say that it is one journey of utterance that acknowledges the boundaries and thresholds of the individual, through and across the nuances and shifts of language and historical time. It draws upon specific discourses and their appeal to knowledge, both provisional and substantive, within the languages of criticism and human sciences and beyond. It is a poetic utterance that looks back to the earliest epic and founding literature and forward beyond any post-modernist position. It has enlarged the focus of the poet beyond the reference frames registered by Ezra Pound's *The Cantos* and Charles Olson's *The Maximus Poems*. It appeals to a community of speakers, readers and writers, cognizant of the fact that all are in a series of markets and hierarchies of language and discourse outlays, without privilege.

This work is substantially supported by critical essays, such as 'Stars, Tigers and the Shape of Words' (The William Matthews Lectures 1992, Birkbeck 1993), where Prynne reassessed the arbitrariness that Ferdinand de Saussure famously attributed to the signifier and signified and emphasized a set of secondary relations through which meaning developed such as historical contexts and usages, accumulated layers and aspects of association, social function and usage codes, and practical criticism, such as *They That Haue Powre To Hurt: A Specimen of a Commentary on Shake-speares Sonnets, 94* (Cambridge 2001) and *Field Notes: The Solitary Reaper And Others* (Cambridge 2007, distributed by Barque Press) that shows an exceptional regard to determining the fullest context and meaning of a poem. Each word and phrase in a poem has a philological and etymological base that returns the reader to things and the world of which they are a part. The words used enact and sustain the relations and forces between language and the world.

In my position as editor of *Tears in the Fence* literary magazine I have received a number of letters about the work of J.H. Prynne. His work is justly seen as impressive but refusing any clear meaning for many readers. I usually reply that *The White Stones* (1969) has a sufficiently wide register and echo, with part of its roots deep in the Book of Revelation, William Blake and the *Lyrical Ballads*, to keep readers moving back and forth for decades to come and that a good start is to look at the words and phrases you recognise, assess the range of their meaning, look at the associations and connections that come to mind, and start asking questions of each word, phrase and line. Two words invariably used to describe the initial experience of reading the poems are 'arid' and 'difficult'. 'Arid', as if it were written in a desert. That is to say that it is often missing the props of mainstream metaphorical poetry that enables a quick grasp of meaning, intention and the scope of the poem under review. It is what is called 'difficult' poetry. It is, as it were, poetry of the desert. I shall now pursue these two notions as a way of locating the literary context to the *Poems*.

Poetry written from the desert, of whatever order, may be seen as poetry of exile. One thinks of Ovid, Paul and Jane Bowles, and the post-holocaust poetry of Edmund Jabès and Paul Celan. The critic, T.W. Adorno wrote that "after Auschwitz, we can no longer write poetry." It was Jabès who wrote that "after Auschwitz, we must write poetry, but with wounded words" and in conversation with the American writer Mark C. Taylor, who said: "It is very hard to live with silence. The real silence is death and this is terrible. To approach this silence, it is necessary to journey into the desert. You do not go into the desert to find identity, but to lose it, to lose your personality, to become anonymous. You make yourself void. You become silence. And something extraordinary happens: you hear silence speak".[1] Further exiled or self-imposed exiled poetry has a social position and ʼ ry effect. By dint of being outside the social-literary mainstream, ore able to comment inwards on the prevailing socio-political ᵔns. One thinks of the ability of Anna Akhmatova's poetry to comment upon Stalinist Russia and the purges and so on. Prynne's poetry, like Jabès and Akhmatova, may be seen in broad moral and literary terms as a profound reaction to the historic events of the twentieth century.

JH Prynne's social-literary position can be seen as a self-imposed exile. He has been, for example, excluded from such literary reference books as *The Oxford Companion to English Literature* edited by Margaret Drabble (OUP 2000) and taken moral decisions on the integrity of how and where his poetry and criticism appears.

His exact social-literary position is complex, given its exile status. Born in 1936, Jeremy Prynne was raised in Kent and educated at Cambridge University. His mother ran a nursery school for boys and girls up to the age of seven and his father was an engineer. At Cambridge he met the poet and critic, Donald Davie, who supported Prynne's early intellectual direction. Like Davie, this was a move away from the insular concerns of the Movement to the richer intellectual concerns of new American and European poetry. Davie's study, *Thomas Hardy And Modern Poetry* (1973) offers an early account of Prynne's early poetry. Previously College Librarian and University Reader in English Poetry and now a Life Fellow at Gonville & Caius College, Cambridge, and currently Hon. Professor of English, University of Sussex, and Visiting Professor at Sun Yat-sen University, China, he works on all aspects of the English poetic tradition, including writings of American, European and Far Eastern origin. In his teaching capacity, his enthusiasm for sharing and generosity of spirit towards many students is well known and helped to develop a wide readership base. However, this is only part of the story. Prynne's poetry emerged as part of an avant-garde discussion and readership outside of the literary market place. An early indication of this can be seen in issue 6 of *Prospect* magazine, edited by Prynne in 1964, containing poems by Dorn, Olson, Crozier, amongst other items, which announces on the back cover:

'*Prospect* will appear four times a year, if writing is offered which will make this worth while and if funds can be found. Only a very small number of copies will be for sale over a counter; but copies will be sent free of charge to any person who, out of a real sense of interest, thinks it worth writing to the editor to ask for them. If libraries wish to subscribe, on the other hand, the charge for four issues is four pounds, sterling or twelve dollars. Work sent in should preferably be extensive enough to define its own contour; thus, groups of poems will stand more firmly than short isolated pieces.'

Later he was responsible for the mimeographing and distribution of *The English Intelligencer*, a literary newsletter, between January 1966 and April 1968. Based in Cambridge and edited by Andrew Crozier in its first series, Peter Riley in its second series, J.H. Prynne edited one issue and Tom Raworth produced a spoof issue of this seminal publication. The third series was assembled rather than edited by Crozier and Prynne.[2] *The English Intelligencer* was an attempt to organise a new collective poetics that focussed upon producing 'quality' work. Drawing upon a wide range of literary and non-literary sources, it was distributed for free to an expanding mailing list. Poems, essays and comments were shared without cost and exchange value. *The Intelligencer* occupied a space somewhere between a private letter and public book and embodied a shared community opposition to market commodification.

J.H. Prynne was a key figure in its articulation of the language and poetics of 'quality' and 'landscape', two key words used in opposition to the language of commodity. His early work, which appeared in *The English Intelligencer*, opens out the wider meanings of key words in the development of counter-poetics. Essentially he wanted to rescue a concept of 'quality' from its financial meaning to make it viable outside of a purely market lexicon. The word 'commodity', for example, has three sources of meaning, commodity as ownership (who owns it, OED 1-4), worth (its exchange value, OED 6) and property (its use, OED 5). The word 'quality' equally has a range of meaning from the degree of excellence of a thing (OED1) to the general and specific attributes of a thing or product (OED 2–3) and the relative nature, kind or character of a thing (OED 4). Other meanings include the distinctive timbre of a voice or sound (OED 5), the archaic meaning of high social standing, as in people of quality (OED 6) and the property of a proposition (OED 7). Since the sixties, of course, the meaning has been extended to imply reduction of variability or compliance with specifications as in 'quality management' and fitness for use or value to a person, both derived from economic origins. When such a word is used the reader is required to assess the range of possible meaning called into play. In the poem, 'Sketch For A Financial Theory of the Self' which first appeared in Series 1 no.17, Prynne probes the relationship between word (name) and object within the economic field and suggests the ways it impacts on the self. He writes of how words and poems and quality, as habit, have been reduced to monetary objects by which we define ourselves. He notes that we are duped into a reductive cash flow nexus: 'The absurd trust in value is the pattern of / bond and contract and interest −' and 'Music, / travel, habit and silence are all money; purity / is a glissade into the last, most beautiful return.' Prynne extended and widened the thinking of quality and money with 'A Note On Metal' (*The English Intelligencer* second series June 1967, appended to *Aristeas* (1968).[3] Here quality is seen in terms of property (strength) and substance. He looks back to the origins of money as coin (gold) and Western alchemy, defined as 'the theory of quality as *essential*'. He differentiates between early Asiatic socio-economic formations where coins were the ornament of power rather than currency of value and early Greek economies where it is the substance governing transfer as exchange. This thinking is further extended and brought historical up to date in the poem, 'Die a Millionaire' from *Kitchen Poems* (1968), where 'the twist-point / is "purchase" − what the mind / bites on is yours' . . . 'we are the social strand / which is *already* past the twist-point & / into the furnace' . . . so that what *I am* is a special case of / what *we want*, the twist-point missed exactly / at the nation's scrawny neck.'[4]

The *English Intelligencer* by removing a formal ownership and exchange value thus produced a newsletter divorced from the literary market. In so doing, they showed that words and poems, as objects, have properties beyond their meanings and exchange value within the community. This move can be seen as an extension of the work and thinking of the Objectivist Press and poets, such as Charles Oppen, Charles Reznikoff and Louis Zukofsky, who searched for a language outside of the ideology and practice of commodification. *The English*

ligencer showed that words and poems could be produced outside
c. commodification and retain intrinsic value for its readership.[5]

The English Intelligencer fostered an intense interest in a wide
range of poetries and philosophy. These included Ezra Pound and
the Imagists, William Carlos Williams and the poetry of things, the
Objectivist poets, such as Oppen et al, the Black Mountain College
poets, such as Olson, Edward Dorn and Robert Duncan, the San
Francisco Renaissance including novelists, William Burroughs and
Jack Kerouac, the New York poets, such as Frank O'Hara and John
Ashbery and the European post-Holocaust poets, such as Jabès and
Celan. Beyond that flux of alternative poetries, Prynne continued his
readings within the English tradition, especially the Romantic poets
and Elizabethan poets and dramatists, and within modern European
philosophy, including Hegel, Wittgenstein, Heidegger, Merleau-Ponty
and the issues of language, being and the phenomenology of perception
raised by their work. Amongst the questions that this reading raised
would be around the notion of the autonomy of the text and whether
there is a singleness and moral structure to immediate knowledge.[6]

Against a backdrop of growing disenchantment with the Vietnam
War, civil disobedience in relation to women's issues, gay issues
environmental issues, industrial strife, a balance-of-trade deficit that
led to the devaluation of the pound and student 'revolt into style',
structuralism moved across from linguistics and anthropology cutting
into sociological, historical, philosophical, psychiatric and critical
thought, with the concept of the de-centred subject and de-centring
of the structure impacting on thinking within European human
sciences. Doubtless buoyed by E.P. Thompson's articulation of the
impact of literary, satirical and political presses in the early nineteenth
century in *The Making of the English Working Class* (1968) and Jeff
Nuttall's overview of more recent oppositional publishing and culture
in *Bomb Culture* (1968), several *English Intelligencer* contributors became
small press publishers. It was through these regional activists that J.H.
Prynne chose to publish most of his early work, beginning with *Day
Light Songs* (Resuscitator Books, Pampisford, Cambridgeshire, 1968),
Aristeas (Ferry Press, London, 1968), *The White Stones* (Grossteste
Press, Lincoln, 1969) and *Fire Lizard* (Blacksuede Boot Press, Barnet,
Hertfordshire, 1970).

The English Intelligencer was never a specifically Cambridge grouping and always looked to deepen understanding of the processes and conditions of the literary. It should be noted that Prynne was active in introducing talented younger poets and writers from outside the University, notably the journalists, Douglas Oliver and Barry MacSweeney, into the circle of information and communication. Its ethos continued in private correspondence between contributors and through private and public publication.

Prynne's early readership then consisted of friends, the avant-garde poets, intellectuals and critics associated with *The English Intelligencer*, his colleagues and students.

The nature of his communication with that growing readership took the form of his poetry and a contribution to the thinking and reading of that audience. It always already posits a literary-social position in relation to a mode of poetic communication that involves questioning before and beyond any current ideology of text, authorship, intention and process of marketing and entails a wandering across and through both language and the literary canon. Over time he deepens and widens that range, by attempting not to suppress variable meaning and knowledge that impinge upon a thing, so that the reader might question various knowledge thresholds, in particular such concepts as 'totality' and 'immediate experience' and 'textual autonomy'.

I shall now turn to the notion of 'difficulty'. This familiar notion in the poetry world is encountered in the first line of the first poem, the magically sonic, 'The Numbers': 'The whole thing it is, the difficult'. A note to the 1982 edition of *Poems* (Allardyce Barnett Books) referred to 'difficulty as being the ardent matter and accompanying breadth of imaginative and political reference'. In other words, it is inherent in the matter addressed as the forces and relations of production and consumption already taint the nuances of languages and knowledge. There is no impartial discourse. 'Difficulty', though, is not misleading, that is to say the reader is either able to grasp something or not. It perhaps implies that the conflicting and impartial knowledge at work is beyond the reach of one reader and some of these poems are beyond comprehension, through the uncertainty of variable meaning. However, it should, at least, be seen as relative and in relation to 'simplicity'.

A seemingly transparent and simple poetic text, such as William Blake's poem 'The Tyger', may require considerable critical work in disentangling the complexity of discourses, method and intentionality and possible effects registered, in the same way as a 'difficult' poem as so much of its sub-text is out of view. This can perhaps be described as 'subtlety' in all its guises. Both 'difficult' and 'simple' poems demand intellectual work and are initially conditioned by prejudicial readings and the disposition towards response and effect. In other words, some poems produce effects and reference knowledge that are unseen or unread by certain readers and that is governed by the reading history and preferences as much as ability of the reader. An awareness of that history, conditioned as it is by ethnic, social, educational, psychological and other factors, and its prejudice, may help dissolve some of weariness generated by poems that refuse to be read. At the macro-level, it might help readers appreciate the divide between those who read poems as language only and those who read poems as social process only and show the need to resist closure on either side of the fence. 'Difficulty' can be distinguished from 'subtlety', meaning that which is not obvious in any way, possessing small and important data, often implying cleverness through its ability to withhold and disguise. Subtlety, then, wants to be acknowledged rather than seen. Difficulty, in contrast, has an intrinsic value in the sense that a poem retains its vitality over time, as in the case of Wordsworth's 'Lucy' poems, and implies an openness or opening towards the complex. It is potentially much less elitist than a work of subtlety.

Whenever poetic effects appear less clear and open the level of difficulty gives rise to anxiety and resistance. However, the reader may recognise a phrase or something from a literary predecessor. The poem 'Lashed to the Mast' from *The White Stones*, may well remind the reader of Odysseus bound by his oarsmen to the mast of his ship, in Book 10 of *The Odyssey*, so that he can hear the song of the Sirens.[7] An examination of the type of vocabulary, its possible connections and associations, set a framework from which to develop a reading. The reader might then ask is the poem in the form of an argument, a revelation or amplification of a state, condition or property, however refracted, and determine the nature of the ordered vocabulary of perceptions and utterances. The reader's critical tools finally rest with each word and its possible meanings in relation to other words, phrases and lines. In Prynne's poetry there are sudden juxtapositions and enjambments that push the thought process and association further along and cut away provisional initial readings. The reader, then, may assume all possible meanings and shifts of meaning are implied until some options can be discarded as illogical or unlikely. The location of these meanings within their historical, financial, commercial, philosophical or scientific origins may shed further light. For example, Prynne's employment of the word, brass, in the collection, *Brass* (1971) immediately covers the seven main meanings of the word and there may well be material that touches upon each of these definitions and elements of the historical and linguistic origin.

The arc of Prynne's poetry may be seen as moving further into exile, a deepening of the challenge to the reader, as a method of registering wider referents, on the basis that this might be a focal point of social and ethical or literary change. Consider the examples of Blake and Kafka, as psychological exiles, self-imposed or not, and the ways their work has entered the language. Now consider, at the micro-level, the individual forced by exceptional circumstances, e.g. the loss of several high school friends to suicide, into self-imposed exile, who returns and begins to campaign for social change in the local community. Consider also a woman who is sexually abused, attacked and raped or the female vagrant. This is a possible territory called into reference by *Her Weasels Wild Returning* (1994),[8] where there are a series of explicit journeys out and back by the poem's implied participants. What happens in these examples is a journey out to exile and a journey back, in altered state, with its concomitant changes. Of course, we should remember that the exiled do not return to exactly the same place as time has elapsed since they left. In a way this is akin to the experience of reading Prynne's poetry.

Interestingly Prynne has spoken of a poetry that journeys out and back. It is a poetic and critical example that clearly informs Prynne's method of composition and reading. Prynne reads Charles Olson's *Maximus Poems IV, V, VI* as having set 'the literal founding of history and its local cadence into speech extend outwards by feeling into the sacral and divinised forms of presence upon the earth's surface' and established as primary writing, 'with a lingual and temporal syncretism, poised to make a new order'. In other words it places language as a mythological likeness resting on the earth through geological time and the *monogene* which 'reaches back into two entwined histories: the geochronology of land-formation and the cytochronology or biochemical evolution'.[9]

In his 1971 Simon Fraser University lectures on *Maximus Poems IV, V, VI*, Prynne delineates that poetry which moved beyond the metaphorical lyric into the epic, offering a reading of the canon, from Homer to Olson via Bruno, Milton, Wordsworth, Blake, Keats and Pound, from that perspective. Obscure epics failed, he notes, as they were freighted down with information and the reader is unable to follow the journey. To be successful the epic must be clear and simple. He equates the homecoming of *Maximus IV, V, VI* with that other epic of homecoming The Odyssey and argues that the poem brings in the cosmos, that is knowledge of the universe considered as a whole. At the beginning of *Maximus IV, V, VI* the narrative turns back from the sea, by which the narrator, for Prynne, means space and the large condition of the cosmos. For Olson to look from the Gloucester coast out into the Atlantic is to look into the whole economic support of early New England settlement and to look back to the mid-Atlantic ridges, which figure in his imagination as the last residues of the birth of the great continents in the original orogenies which formed the earth. Olson then has an outward journey and an inward journey, stretching lyricism into epic through the folding back of the voyage out. Prynne argues that each of the fragments of *Maximus* participates in the whole so that it is literal and not an insistence of something else and therefore escapes metaphor. As such this leads to a condition of being, which is beyond the condition of meaning. The arc of the *Maximus* poem is a singular and circular journey out to the limits of space and back to local historical roots achieved as a curvature that moves beyond the lyric into the condition of myth.[10]

Olson believed that poetry exists in an open-field through which the poet transmits energy to the receptive reader. His work encompassed myth, history, geology and politics, all marked by the curiosity and openness to experience that he asked of his readers.

Ralph Maud's *A Charles Olson Reader* (Carcanet, 2005) provides an excellent introduction to his life and work. Prynne and *The English Intelligencer* poets absorbed Olson's poetry and essays, especially 'Projective Verse' (1950) and 'Human Universe' (1959) as a revitalising and energising movement. Olson's insistence on cutting the poetic line according to one's breath, that a poem should be a high energy-construct and discharge, that form is never more than an extension of content, and one perception must immediately and directly lead to a further perception clearly impacted upon the *English Intelligencer* poets. Olson wrote 'It is by their syllables that words juxtapose in beauty, by these particles of sound as clearly as by the sense of the words which they compose'[11] Prynne and Raworth in particular have been inspired by this thinking about sound and sense.

Olson provided Prynne with a modern epic template, of the journey out and back, and of poetry that places language on earth in geophysical time through the monogene. Prynne has extended this model into a reading experience that is uniquely his own, redolent with acute vocabularies and terse energy points. He offers encounters with language and the various discourses that impinge upon the individual showing how the individual is formed by processes that are outside immediate perception and cognition. His movement beyond metaphorical language seems to be entirely consistent with the scope of his initial enquiries and an attempt to find a more adequate measure of discursive pressures. Recurrent figures and sound patterns replace normative narratives. The use of juxtaposition and enjambment to move seamlessly from one thought or perception to another is done, as Olson advised, at speed so as to bring seeming disparate discourses or elements of discourses into the sphere of activity being registered. Olson's impact on Prynne is most noticeable in his early work, especially *The White Stones*, which can be read, in part, as an investigation of the transfer of language to the human account. It is Olson's 'Human Universe' essay that forms a backbone to the collection's frame of reference.

In this essay Olson saw all post-Socratic philosophy as a false discourse of logic, classification and idealism, as opposed to a discourse that takes language as an action upon the real. 'We have lived long in a generalizing time, at least since 450 BC' he wrote and went to distinguish between 'language as the act of the instant and language as the act of thought about the instant' (12) To Olson, Aristotelian logic and classification have fastened themselves on habits of thought so that action is absolutely interfered with. In other words, the habits of thought are the habits of action, collapsing language from an instrument into an absolute with the Greeks declaring all speculation as enclosed in the 'universe of discourse'. Olson calls for a writing that does not fall back 'on the dodges of discourse', a demonstration, a separating out, a classification. 'For any of us, at any instant, are juxtaposed to any experience, even an overwhelming single one, on several more planes than the arbitrary and discursive which we inherit can declare'.[13] (This surely could stand as a preface to the work of Prynne's *Poems*.) Olson further notes that a thing impinges upon us by self-existence, without reference to any other thing, by its particularity that is to be found beyond reference and description and wants to bear in rather than away from a thing so as to discover and reveal.

Olson's *Maximus* and 'Human Universe' essay, combined with Homer's epic *The Odyssey*, leads Prynne and the reader to consider the exile in terms of the founding moment of historical self-awareness and, at the same time, as the site of various philosophical and individual splits and boundaries. It is the exile posited on the material foundation of historical change or reinstatement and displaced from any singular viewpoint. By challenging our ordinary linguistic ordering of the world, beginning with an analysis of concept formation in the financial world, Prynne's poetry makes us question the way in which we make sense of things.

Notes

[1] Edmond Jabès *The Book of Margins*, Trans. Rosmarie Waldrop. Chicago: University of Chicago Press, 1993.

[2] Nate Dorward *J.H. Prynne: A Checklist*, www.ndorward.com December 2004.

[3] J.H. Prynne *Poems*. Tarset: Bloodaxe Books, 2005 pp.127–132.

[4] *Ibid* pp.13–16.

Mass Production: The Quality of the Word: Dan Friedman *Left : Review*, 2002, www.leftbankreview.com pp.28–33.

[6] For a discussion of these issues see Kevin Nolan: 'Capital Calves: Undertaking an Overview'. *Jacket* 24, www.jacket.com November 2003 pp.1–37.

[7] *Ibid* p.1.

[8] J.H. Prynne *Poems* 2005 especially pp.412–416.

[9] J.H. Prynne: 'Charles Olson, Maximus IV,V,VI', *The Park* 4 & 5 Summer 1969 pp.64–66.

[10] 'Minutes of the Charles Olson Society' No 28 April 1999 pp.3–13. www.charlesolson.ca/files/Prynnelecture.

[11] Ralph Maud (ed.): *A Charles Olson Reader*, Carcanet Press, Manchester, 2005 p.41.

[12] *Ibid* p.113.

[13] *Ibid* p.114.

DRAWING ON PRYNNE:
TACIT CONVERSATIONS WITH IAN FRIEND AND HIS WORK

Richard Humphreys

Covent Garden offers many delights, but none so deep and lasting as an experience at Inner Space. This meditation and self-development centre offers an oasis of peace to shoppers, office workers, visitors and others. All you need is a few minutes to spare, and an interest in touching base with the real, peaceful self.

(From the website for 'Inner Space—The Breathing Space', www.innerspace.com, 2005)

Innerspace has access to a wide variety of equipment such as sidescan sonar and towfish specialized for both deep and shallow water applications, magnetometers, remote operated vehicles, underwater video and still cameras.

(From the website for 'Innerspace Exploration Team', www.innerspacexploration.com, 2005)

In darkness by day we must press on,
giddy at the tilt of a negative crystal.
(J.H. Prynne 'The Oval Window', 1982)[1]

Somewhere else in the market

From the heart of the city to the depths of the ocean, we are haunted in our nervy, crumbling lives by the thought or half-hint of the discovered or recovered heart of things—that is to say, perhaps, our selves. Over the last hundred years or so artists have sought to make images explicitly suggestive of that ambiguous and debatable cavern zone we may refer to as 'inner space', a dangerously irresistible chamber of secrets now common parlance in soft New Age and hard scientific and technological contexts alike. Of course, one might say that most, even all, visual art to some degree cannot avoid doing this, as subjective and objective realities are in image-making such osmotic and interactive spheres; you are always witnessing in art some form of mutual spillage between them. Whether it is a medieval manuscript or Rubens's fleshpots, Turner's storms or Cézanne's mountain, there is no possibility of some simply objective representation which does not include the rich and paradoxical presence of human perception and lurking consciousness. However, the complex intellectual and cultural histories which from the late nineteenth century made a self-conscious awareness of our specifically mental space a central concern of many artists, can be traced in, among other forms, Cubist, Futurist, Surrealist and abstract art right through to the varied practice of artists today. The uncertainty attached to investigating such a hidden and uncanny phenomenological and metaphysical zone brings with it dangers and opportunities which only a few have successfully exploited.

Where is this 'space'? How do we account for it and what would it mean to make it the subject of painting? Is it something we can 'see' as we 'see' a table and chair in front of us? Is it something we invent from a few scraps and clues, dreams and intimations? I close my eyes and 'see' a darkness with a host of murky shapes, from brief after-images to recurring forms for which there is little hard evidence of origins. This may become a swimmingly evocative stage or backdrop for more or less strong fantasy in which I create, or have some sense of creating, any number of figures and structures. The primary means of capturing something of this perilously unstable country in the twentieth century was 'automatism', derived from psychoanalytic, symbolist and occultist procedures and first theorised, through Freudian contexts, in ways which became available to a wide experimental cultural audience by the Surrealists in the 1920s. Taking their cue from the initial efforts of poets, painters such as André Masson and Joan Miró developed different means of tapping into submerged thoughts and images which, in the process of dredging, became distinctive languages concerned with the articulation of the hidden and sexually numinous. In conventional art historical formulations we then find American artists, or Europeans based in New York, such as Jackson Pollock and Arshile Gorky in the 1940s extending the scale, registers and ambition of these languages. Prynne's own analysis of Willem de Kooning's canvas 'Rosy-Fingered Dawn at Louse Point' (1963) fathoms some of these hermeneutic complexities.[2]

The orthodoxy which unites the different means used by artists from Masson to Pollock and beyond—(Francis Bacon and de

Kooning, both more obviously 'figurative' artists, can be seen to bear strong traces of this)—was a commitment to an idea of spontaneity of process and minimal, though usually significant, editing of the material so produced. Yet with the critical presence of Clement Greenberg breathing down many an artistic neck it has been seen to be in the nature of these essentially 'modernist' practices that, in spite of the darkly psychological and even literary sources of the work, it should be resolutely formal and even classical in its commitment to an abstract integrity.

a picture is not a window

I introduced Ian Friend to Prynne's poetry in between pints of Young's Bitter in a pub on Millbank in the early 1980s and unwittingly set off a trail in his career as an artist which has led him further and further into the unique and variously disturbed and calming inner space of the poet's wordscapes. It all began, during another ridiculous lunch hour, when we found we both loved Frank O'Hara—I had recently produced some of his Off-Off Broadway plays—and, via a purchase of the Agneau2 Prynne volume[3] at a bookshop in Red Lion Square, a few games of cricket involving its proprietor, to Friend's amazed and baffled reaction to Prynne's words. He was drawn by the tremulous screen of precise suggestions which rarely travel dutifully to a fixed point on the horizon. We both responded to the weird range of references, the complete formal control, subtle music and sense of breaking through, in language, to entirely new worlds of experience. Friend began to make drawings in response to the poetry and quickly began a correspondence which, surprisingly, has not yet led to the two men meeting one another, even though they are regularly in touch and Friend made a show around his 'Oval Window' works in 2002 and published a new edition of the poem the same year.

'The Oval Window' draws its title from the physiology of the inner ear. An oval window specifically is a membrane aperture in the middle ear through which sound waves pass to be converted into neural impulses and thereafter transmitted to the brain where the mysterious process of cognitive 'hearing' really takes place. Sounds arrive through the ear drum (the tympanic membrane) deep in the ear canal and make their way via a kind of sinister and Vulcanesque percussive structure of tiny bones, the 'ossicles'—the malleus (hammer), incus (anvil) and stapes (stirrup)—to the oval window. The pressure at this stage is highly concentrated compared with that arriving at the outer ear, thus amplifying the sound waves many times over. Beyond this tiny membranous opening, which is moved in and out by the action of the piston-like stapes, is a fluid in the complex cochlea which causes a vibration wave to travel down the basilar membrane. Behind this basic description of the mechanism there is much strangeness about an area also "central to the construction of verbal language".[4] As one on-line medical textbook has it: "Hearing in general is still very mysterious to us. The basic concepts at work in human and animal ears are fairly simple, but the specific structures are extremely complex. Scientists are making rapid advancements, however, and they discover new hearing elements every year. It's astonishing how much is involved in the hearing process, and it's even more amazing that all these processes take place in such a small area of the body". One instance of the mystery is the phenomenon of 'reverse' hearing; in one recent case a patient complained of persistent whispering in the ear apparently caused by the basilar membrane 'hitting' the oval window, the stapes, through to the eardrum where a doctor heard it with a stethoscope. We are at a point where the techniques of different observers seem to interact—the microscopist, the x-ray technician, the ear specialist and visionary psychoanalyst. Poets and artists might well choose to occupy a similar set of vantage points.

It is not surprising, then, that a poet, particularly one with Prynne's scientific interests, might be so fascinated by this aspect of human function. For an artist it is a little more surprising; why not consider the mechanisms of sight? That isn't necessary of course, but an added interest to a visual artist reading *The Oval Window* is that Prynne also invokes the actions of the so-called 'snowdrift line', the tiny calcite crystals which lie loosely packed on the otoconial membranes of the inner ear. As Neil Reeve and Richard Kerridge put it in their brilliant reading of the poem: "These crystals are responsible for providing the brain with information as to the position of the head within the earth's gravitational field. They begin to develop around the tenth week of gestation, and by the twenty-sixth week are virtually fully formed. Sending impulses to the brain at a prenatal stage when the eye and the auditory ear are still quite limited in their functions . . . The otoconial mass does not form itself into a finished state which then remains unaltered throughout life. It constitutes instead a continuously developing system of combinations and replacements whose end is to measure and promote the stability of the organism . . . David Hubbard, a follower of Schilder's pioneering work on the role of gravitational awareness in the formation of human personality . . . saw the otolith crystals as 'physical particles which symbolically represent the outer world'. They comprise the 'organ' through which 'gravity speaks'. The suggestion seems to be that, by registering the laws of gravity upon the human brain, the crystals act as agents for a primal encounter with external reality, a negative point or limit for the ego's aspirations (in this case, to fly or to float)"[5]. This seems very suggestive and, for a visual artist concerned with inside and outside and with R.S. Thomas's 'wound of knowledge', a way into a graphic interpretation of the edges of self and not-self. (I also think, incidentally, of a multiplying, even paranoid, 'crowd' in looking at these forms). As Reeve and Kerridge say, the "crystals, for example, could be said virtually to constitute the point where mind and matter start to intertwine".[6] Hubbard's mentor, the investigator of 'body image', Paul Schilder, was important for one of Prynne's own intellectual sources, the phenomenological philosopher Maurice Merleau-Ponty. And his ideas can be linked to those of one of Ian Friend's most important sources, Gaston Bachelard's *The Poetics of Space*, where the poetical French phenomenologist talks of space as containing "compressed time". In this instance "inner space", where the philosopher's notion of the metaphysical being at the interface between the "reverberation" of the work of art and the "resonance" of recognition of the viewer. Ian Friend explicitly refers to his richly ambiguous drawings as "concerned with gravity, balance and a sense of simultaneous interiority/exteriority".[7] There are intimations of many visual sources in the drawings, from Holbein to Ben Nicholson. In the artist's own words: "They examine quite explicitly concepts fundamental to early 20th century practice and the development of abstraction as a vehicle for the speculative and poetic imagination. The works attempt to manifest the intangible through the abstract yet very material act of drawing. That it is work on paper that constitutes the final statement, asserts the primacy of a medium that has tended to be viewed as a preliminary statement, enquiry or exploration subservient to a 'finished' resolution in painting, sculpture or other form".[8] The 'bio-morphic' art of Arp and early Rothko is part of Friend's tradition; but so is Australian aboriginal art, Bellini and Vermeer.

Friend's drawings are ambitiously large pieces in both physical size and aesthetic and intellectual scope and the forms of ovals and circles, great oceans of grey and wash, delicate bone shapes and crystal drifts, have a beauty, grace and depth of presence lacking in so much art today. They demand close attention and absorption. The artist continues: "The works are made over a significant time frame and demand the same effort from the viewer. This is quite specific in intent as the works offer a philosophical position of the value of contemplation given the frenetic nature of many aspects of life in the twentieth century. It is hoped that the works offer themselves as a vehicle for penetrating surfaces to unveil unseen but palpable truths".[9]

and the end is hazy like the meaning

Ian Friend was born in the county of Sussex, England, the spiritual home of chalky works on paper I like to think, and moved to the new possibilities offered by the expanses of Australia in 1985 where he has lived and practised ever since. Having worked for many years as a sculptor, from 1993 he has produced work on paper only. Much of his work since 1997 has the generic title 'Metaphysics' and is organised in sets which now number seven. There are also related series, for instance 'For JHP', drawing on his responses to Prynne. As the artist writes "all of the works investigate the possibility of a metaphysical experience expressed through an abstract process. It is a diachronic body of work, the result of an allusive relationship to history, poetry, speculation, memory and reverie".[10] He is aware of the dangers of performing illustration in relation to Prynne's work, but he has avoided this by pursuing his own imaginative direction and working methods. As Prynne said in a letter to Friend in connection with a "breathtaking package" of a small work he had just received from Friend: "I am so thrilled to have it . . . what is so satisfying (about No.18) is its unemphatically confident resistance to stories about itself, or seriality or allegation of any kind."[11]

What follows are some simple questions and pondered responses conducted by e-mail, mail, phone call and some degree of telepathy between London and Brisbane. Most of the specific references are to 'The Oval Window', the poem Friend has engaged with most frequently and profoundly over the years.

RH: Which volume of Prynne's did you read first?

IF: The big paperback *Poems* published by Agneau2 in 1982. I liked the plain cream cover and minimal text. I bought it at Duck Soup in Lamb's Conduit Passage near Red Lion Square. It was Nick Kimberley's bookshop. We used to play cricket against him when I captained the Tate Gallery team. He was a pretty useful left arm finger spinner. I can remember (over twenty years ago) batting against him and being completely bamboozled by him once. He made a terrible mess of my stumps.

RH: What was it you particularly liked about that cover?

IF: I liked the relationship between the text and the space of the cover. It may in some way have reminded me of the economy of the Penguin paperback edition of Joyce's *Ulysses*—do you remember, the black one with the white text? Yes, it was the economy of design I liked.

RH: What did you make of the poetry at that moment of introduction?

IF: I read it from cover to cover and quite honestly I can say I was a bit bamboozled by Prynne, much like Kimberley's spinners. I couldn't pretend that I understood the layerings in the poems initially. Sometimes it felt as if the language deliberately resisted interpretation, thereby emphasising the language. At other times a genuine lyricism was beguiling. But I knew there was something there which absolutely captivated me, so I read all of the poems in that volume again, trying not to worry about certain expectations about what constituted poetry.

RH: Well, Prynne is a mind-boggler for most readers at first, and maybe always should be. Can you give some examples of lines you like and suggest what it is that 'gets' you? 'The Oval Window' might be the place to look—I'm not trying to find exact matches between the poetry and your art, just a taste of how particular sequences of words grab you.

IF: Here are some passages and phrases I especially respond to and have been moved and visually stimulated by:

> 'Being asked to cut
> Into the bone matches wishing to become
> The one that asks and is sharply hurt.'

I also like 'plasma leaking', 'the whole falling short is wounded vantage', 'you let a lifelong transfusion, as by the selfsame hands that made these wounds' and 'How a gang of boys set her face alight with a flaming aerosol can, "her mouth was sealed by the burns"'.

All of them refer to the body and a certain vulnerability in terms of wounds (deliberate) or injury (deliberate or accidental). One of my earliest drawings from Prynne in fact was titled 'The Wound, Day and Night'. The repetition of this imagery is not incidental: it is a deliberate build up to the graphic image of the aerosol can. There is something quite brutal in the imagery created by media reportage, and Prynne knows exactly how to use this in the context of the perimeters, the internal/external body, the evidence of the wound and the possibility of infection.

RH: Can you say a bit more about this?

IF: Compare those lines I've just cited to this later on in the poem:

> Her wrists shine white like the frosted snow:
> They call each other to the south stream.
> The oval window is closed in life,
> By the foot-piece of the stapes. Chill shadows
> Fall from the topmost eaves, clear waters
> Run beside the blossoming peach.

This is really very beautiful, very lyrical in a Chinese and Poundian way, and compared with the previous lines makes an extraordinary leap of emotional and lyric register which I find compelling.

RH: Why do you find this 'leaping' important?

IF: Prynne has always impressed me with the diversity of his language and sources—it's a trademark I suppose. It can read very lyrically at times, particularly for me in 'The Oval Window', but at other times it is fractured or dislocated and without any traditional beauty to it. Often it makes one work very hard, but I don't mind that at all. I don't mind art being difficult and contradictory, so I suppose I can transfer that attitude to visual art and to my own work.

RH: Can you say a bit more about enjoying art being 'hard'?

IF: Maybe 'hard' is the wrong word. Perhaps 'multi-layered' or 'complex' are more appropriate. I don't like to get the 'story' straightaway. Having said that, I'm certainly not in favour of narrative in art.

RH: Sometimes the 'hardness' is to do with emotional responses too.

IF: Absolutely. The last stanza of 'The Oval Window' is extraordinary.

> Standing by the window I heard it,
> while waiting for the turn. In hot light
> and chill air it was the crossing flow
> of even life, hurt in the mouth but
> exhausted with passion and joy. Free
> to leave at either side, at the fold line

found in threats like herbage, the watch
is fearful and promised before. The years
jostle and burn up as trust plasma.
Beyond help it is joy at death itself:
A toy hard to bear, laughing all night.

I used the phrase 'Joy at Death Itself' as the title of a series of works. This was the time that my mother and father both died within three years of each other, both reaching eighty seven. Of course there is sadness, reflection on a life or lives, but mostly a celebration of life, reflected in my own life with my partner Robyn and our son Dexter. This is all about shift, memory and renewal. It is the difficulty or 'hardness' of emotion and the attempt to find 'poise', to use a suggestive word from the poem.

RH: I'm reminded of Bachelard's idea of 'an ethics of joy'. Can you say something about how reading Prynne's poetry might help you get to a finished work?

IF: I like the density in Prynne's poetry. One is simply aware of a profound intelligence at work. I feel that I am in the presence of an inquiring mind, someone with a curiosity and understanding of a wide range of experience and disciplines. I don't pretend to be in that league intellectually or academically, but I'd like to think that my work is the product of an inquiring and intelligent approach that understands the ramifications of knowledge and in particular of the history and methods and materials of my craft. That sense of inquiry in Prynne urges me on.

RH: The craft is important to both of you, indeed. Can you say something more about the significance of the history of the methods and materials in your work and if you think that links to Prynne.

IF: The idea of craft in art is very important to me. I think it can be a bit of a minefield to compare different disciplines, or to say that a painting or drawing has 'poetic' or 'musical' qualities. When working off some of the concepts presented by poetry it is a dangerous area as it would be easy to lapse into illustration, but maybe without such danger there's no art.

RH: But particular materials are very important in your work.

IF: Certainly. For the past ten years my work has exclusively used paper as the support. I have worked with various combinations of Indian ink, gouache, pure pigment, casein, watercolour, crayon and pencil. Papers I've used have been Arches, Rives, Whatman, Indian Khadi and various Japanese ones. I use aqueous media on paper because it proved to be the right thing for the ideas I was dealing with. At the moment I cannot see any great change happening in the future

The materials I currently use in my work I have found are the most appropriate for the concept. It's basically work on paper, not necessarily classifiable as painting or drawing. That being said I do continue to look at artists who have used paper extensively as a support. I must say that I cannot draw a distinct parallel with Prynne except that belief in the in-depth knowledge of one's medium. The relationship with the history of one's practice cannot be measured in explicit manifestation in that practice. For example, I continue to learn from looking at Holbein's drawings, but you probably would not recognise specific influences in my work. Prynne has no doubt read every significant poem ever written in English. I do not know about his multilingual strengths or otherwise.

RH: I'd assume strengths there too—and now in Chinese! Can you say something about some of your visual sources? I'm thinking about art historical and otherwise.

IF: I was brought up in the 1950s and 1960s in rural Sussex, just outside Eastbourne, and the space of the South Downs landscape I think had quite a profound effect for the rest of my life. I painted that landscape from a young age and I can look at Eric Ravilious's paintings of that landscape and I am immediately transported back. I used to love fishing in the local rivers and from the beach and Eastbourne pier. I think it was as much to do with tranquillity, watching wildlife, the slowly moving dense brown rivers and the changing light and breeze as it was to do with catching fish. Whenever I return to England I try to revisit some of the places I fished.

RH: Thinking of the Downs, your drawing materials and 'The Oval Window' I'm struck by a geological coincidence—the chalk landscape, the white pigment you use and the calcite crystals which form the so-called 'snow drift line' behind the 'oval window' in the inner ear which are referred to in the poem.

IF: That's an interesting connection and one I'd not thought about before. There may be a subliminal connection going on there. The white gouache that I use is Winsor and Newton Permanent White and it is the white pigment I have used for the past ten years (after trying other manufacturer's products extensively). It is extremely flexible in terms of being adaptable to washes and opaque application. It is also very flexible in terms of the processes of accretion and erasure that I apply. I think that in retrospect it does relate to the colour of the chalk pits and the cut figures in the southern chalk downs. (The Long Man of Wilmington, The White Horse of Uffington, The Cerne Abbas Giant—what a wonderful erection!) These figures are very graphically cut into the surface to expose the chalk underneath. I frequently use the white gouache to establish quite graphic forms, and etch through the process of abrasion into surfaces to uncover new forms and reform previous pentimenti.

RH: I can't help thinking Prynne would be fascinated by these convergences of process, material, meaning and geology. (You might also get something from reading H.J. Massingham's 1930s works on the Downs and their meanings). Talking of 'pentimenti', do you ever go back to the poems while working and find yourself making changes?

IF: Prynne referred in a letter he wrote to me a few years ago (1 April 2001) to the relationship between our different efforts as being a 'tacit conversation rather than overt illustration'. I think that says it accurately. The main sequence with which I have had a 'tacit conversation' is 'The Oval Window', and I did revisit the poems frequently, not to find specific phrases but more like touchstones of that fragile barrier of interiority/exteriority that are referenced. In fact, when you make a connection like I did with 'The Oval Window', I don't think you ever lose it. I don't believe in 'closure'. If you have been close to someone and they die you can never achieve 'closure', and why would you want to do that?

RH: Going back to 'The Oval Window', did you go to medical textbooks for the imagery you developed in responding to the poem? I'm wondering in particular about what seem to be the calcite crystals in some of the drawings.

IF: I went to the University of Queensland Medical Library to seek out images of the inner ear, oval window, crystals and so on and more or less drew a blank. The library is excellent but the texts and images that I looked at in respect of the subject were really disappointing. I cannot imagine how any medical student would gain an understanding of the subject from the existing images in such books. All of the works that have the 'cloud' of dots reference the crystals. They are applied by brush or little finger on (initially) wet paper that gradually dries. As the paper dries the dots become more defined. Basically, I invented my own 'snowdrift line'. There is no specific reference but the 'snowdrift line' in the works operates internally/externally, within/outside the body. There is a duality of landscape/body.

RH: 'The Joy at Death Itself' works carry intimations of cellular transformation as well as of the calcite crystals, I think.

IF: Yes, they do. Laurie Duggan, the writer, has noted how the oval shapes and 'snowy' dots get smaller and smaller as the series progresses, "varying greatly in definition, multiplied like cells that could represent growth in benign or malign (cancerous) forms. The works ... celebrate this paradox".[12] And you said of them in an introduction to a show of mine in 2003 that "Cancer cells are strange. They could go one way or another, depending on things that may not just be biochemical. When they get a grip they change everything, inside and outside, effecting a metamorphosis. When someone dies everything changes".[13] That about sums it up for me.

RH: Overall, how would you characterise the impact of Prynne on your art?

IF: He has had an absolutely profound impact on the work. I think it is above all the 'tacit' conversation that is important. As you know, I have made work in response to other poets (Shakespeare, Donne, Apollinaire, Eliot, Heaney, Zbigniew Herbert and others), but this is somehow different. Prynne is a constant irritant—one is not allowed a simple grasp of the complexity of the layers and juxtapositions of language. The irritant in the oyster creates the pearl! I also think that reading Prynne has not only profoundly affected my work but has also redefined my critical engagement with contemporary poetry—no quarter given and no favour asked. My overwhelming feeling is that this work is created in a spirit of generosity. So much is presented that demands response. There is obviously immense and diverse learning at play and, I think, a subtle sense of humour.

Calm waves flow onward to the horizon

I am alerted by the subtle washes and silent scumblings of association in reading back over these responses. There is something like a harmonic visual white noise at play in the drawings, temporally disjointed fathomings and soundings in watery channels of devious inter-connection between the inner and outer worlds. Bachelard speaks of images as 'incapable of repose'. Blake comes to mind, in his great image of Newton for instance, which shows the scientist drowsily inscribing rational thought in his sub-marine study, and in his remarkable invocations of restless bodily powers and psychic trembling; Coleridge's 'Ancient Mariner' and John Livingston Lowe's astonishingly detailed analysis of the sources for that poem, much of it scientific, and indeed aqueously so, in origin; depth-charged etymologies for words such as 'sund', the old English for 'sea' and 'water', and associations with health and safety, wound and trauma, dream and vulnerability. Friend's debt to Ben Nicholson suggests the ideas of Nicholson's friend, the aesthetician Adrian Stokes. Stokes's Kleinian sense of immanent fantasy in evolving form touches my critical nerves somehow in looking at Friend's work, watching how he takes a series of lines, Paul Klee-like, for a sinuous walk through the intimations of the depths and warps of the radiologist's world. Prynne once told me how excited he was by the physical and psychological experience of jet-lag, the sense of disorientation and the opening up of the self to new experience out of the damaged former incarnations left behind across the world. That seems to hint at something of this distant and delicate 'tacit conversation' between him and Ian Friend.

Notes

[1] J.H. Prynne 'The Oval Window', in *Poems*. Tarset: Bloodaxe Books, 2005, p.338.

[2] J.H. Prynne *Poems*, Agneau2 (Allardyce Barnett Publishers), Lewes, 1982.

[3] J.H Prynne 'A Discourse on de Kooning's 'Rosy-Fingered Dawn at Louse Point', given at the de Kooning Symposium, Tate Gallery, London, Friday 5 May, 1995.

[4] Laurie Duggan, Introduction, 'The Oval Window: Ian Friend', Brisbane City Gallery, 2002.

[5] N. H. Reeve and Richard Kerridge, *Nearly Too Much: The Poetry of J.H. Prynne*, Liverpool University Press 1995, pp.153–4).

[6] Ibid. p154.

[7] Ian Friend, Notes to the author, 2005.

[8] Ibid.

[9] Ibid.

[10] Ibid.

[11] J.H. Prynne to Ian Friend, letter, 3 April 1999.

[12] Laurie Duggan, *op.cit.*

[13] Richard Humphreys, *Joy at Death Itself: Ian Friend*, Brisbane, 2003.

J.H. Prynne's Poetry and its Relations with Chinese Poetics

Li Zhimin (黎志敏)

J.H. Prynne's repute as a prominent contemporary poet has been blooming steadily in the West and in the East in recent years. "All the same Prynne's work in this line is the most important in English poetry since Eliot . . ."[1] Yet Prynne is more than a poet merely of the English language for he is familiar with German, French, Italian, Chinese, etc., although he is living and working in England and composing mainly in English. And Prynne's poetry are being translated into all different languages. "In China, a translation of 'Pearls That Were' (only 500 copies of which were produced in England) has sold more than 50,000 copies."[2]

"In an article in *The Times*, 3 December 1987, the novelist, biographer and critic Peter Ackroyd described J.H. Prynne as 'without doubt the most formidable and accomplished poet in England today, a writer who has single-handedly changed the vocabulary of expression'. Here we have a poet hailed as the founder of a new school of writing, whose work offers a radical and important alternative to the mainstream of contemporary British poetry."[3] One might find it a difficult task to understand "a new school" in the traditional way, as Prynne has certainly not deliberately organised any group. As a matter of fact, even if one were interested in following his poetical practice, one might often feel frustrated for lack of necessary academic or poetical background.

I. Prynne and Pound

Prynne, who developed his poetical career in the wake of "the Pound era", to borrow a term from Hugh Kenner, is sometimes found to be connected with Pound in terms of poetics. Considering the fact that Prynne has been giving lectures on Pound at Cambridge University for many years, the poetic connection between Prynne and Pound is very natural. "With the publication—not of a collected or selected edition—but of a substantial volume simply entitled *Poems*, outsiders at last have the opportunity to judge for themselves. The initial—and, for that matter, the final—impression one gets is that of someone rooted resolutely in the modernist tradition. In particular, one is at first reminded of Pound. There is the same opacity and hardness of edge. . . . There is the presence of other languages—no Greek, but snippets of Latin, German, Italian, medieval and renaissance English, and even a page of Chinese characters."[4] To be influenced by Pound does not necessarily mean that Prynne is writing Poundian poetry. Neither can we so easily draw a conclusion that Prynne is a modernist on the basis of his poetical development in the wake of the Modernist Movements in the West, as likewise we cannot classify Prynne as a Romanticist because of his wide reading of William Wordsworth's poetical works. Alan Halsey pointed out some difference between Prynne and Pound. "Pound too is a difficult poet: do Pound and Prynne present similar difficulties? . . . once Pound's method and means of assembly have been grasped, the principal difficulty of the *Cantos* is one of reference. A *Canto* is, as it were, a node of references all of which point *outside* the poem—and which for all Pound's skill do implacably remain outside the poem. The reader gains some slight advantage from this, since it means that he can clarify many obscurities simply by reference to the relevant source-material; . . . It does not, we might say, manage to subsume its source-material within itself, to present or re-present it in the mesh of its surface. It is arguable that this is what the best of Prynne's work does achieve, if on a smaller scale than the *Cantos* intended . . . His [Prynne's] writing is a work of much greater compression than Pound's; we must follow his demand that we observe its confines and the 'signals' the page presents, which will guide us within rather than outside itself."[5]

In fact Prynne's scholarship in many fields outgrew that of Pound such as in the field of Chinese poetics, concerning which Pound left many defects in his works, which are not repeated in Prynne's works. Recent critics have pointed out the limitation of Pound's ideas about Chinese poetics: "The point that Prynne stresses throughout his essay is that conventional Western ideas about Chinese lyrics, ideas largely derived from Pound, are not appropriate to the Jade Terrace anthology."[6] In commenting on Anne Birrell's translation of some classical Chinese poems, Prynne concluded after a very detailed and insightful explication: "To this extent they are a scholar's translation, rather than those of a poet. But they assist towards a clearer understanding, as perhaps no poet's version easily could, of what in that distant culture the idea and practice of poetry actually was; not, as Waley implied, something already half-familiar nor, as Pound suggested, an instrument for defamiliarising the too easily recognised, but something of extreme interest which is presented so as to be accessible, while at the same time preserving an almost complete independence of the motive in Western readers to appropriate on our own terms." [7]

Prynne is stronger than Pound in many academic and poetical fields although he surely has benefited from Pound; on the other hand, Pound might also be stronger than Prynne in some fields: a larger discussion is beyond the scope of this essay.

II. Prynne's Poetical Characteristics

Despite the fact that there has been more or less a decline of widespread attention to poetry in the twentieth century, there has always been a constant exploration, and hence development, in the poetical field in England. It is not exaggerated to say that English poetry has made a lot of progress since the Modernist Movement. "Perhaps I can only venture to say that the current poetry scene in Britain demands renewed attention from readers and critics alike because, on its relatively small but widely varied, internationalized stage, it is richly enacting the breakdown of older orders and newly responding to the sorts of post-colonial and post-patriarchal as well as 'post-modern' instillations that have in differing vocabularies spelled the fates of many other cultural/political structures in our *fin-de-siècle* world." [8] Prynne has remained a prominent figure in this current, but not necessarily as a "post-modernist".

Unlike Pound who enjoyed a somewhat wider popularity when composing, Prynne is not "popular". "One thing which can be said with certainty about the poetry of J.H. Prynne is that it is decidedly non-popular and that the poet has never been in any danger of that kind of corruption, even if he has a large reputation in certain circles." [9] It may even seem very likely that the poet himself has deliberately created the unpopularity of his poems; one of his ways is to limit the distribution of his works. "All of Prynne's poetry from Kitchen Poems onwards (Cape Goliard, 1968) was published by 'small presses' or self-published, often in beautifully designed formats."[10] Prynne might have been resisting a move to become "popular", distinguishing himself from the pop-media that have been chasing popularity and fame, causing a rocketing production of merely fashionable publications.

In order to create sensational effects and make money, pop-media often do not mind pandering to the public, and by doing so, creating a low standard of taste in the public. As a poet, Prynne insists that a reader should work to understand and enjoy a piece of artistic work, and by doing so, to develop more complex powers of responsiveness, such as intelligence, imagination, aesthetic judgment, a good poetical taste and so on. This is one important reason why Prynne would not be an "easy" poet, as Eliot advocated many years ago: "We can only say that it appears likely that poets in our civilization, as it exists at present, must be *difficult*. Our civilization comprehends great variety and complexity, and this variety and complexity, playing upon a refined sensibility, must produce various and complex results. The poet must become more and more comprehensive, more allusive, more indirect, in order to force, to dislocate if necessary, language into his meaning."[11]

As Veronica Forrest-Thomson worked on a poem by Prynne—'Of Sanguine Fire'—more than twenty years ago, she well experienced the difficulty of understanding such compositions: "They are tendentiously obscure. They resist the reader by making him work; they positively repel him by implying that no amount of arcane knowledge will help him produce an interpretation, that however hard he tries he will not get away with (or through) these lines into a non-poetic realm. He will have to recognise that he is stuck with the lines on the page, that these words have a meaning but not an extended reference to the world outside, and that his limitation/expansion will have to take place within the levels of the poem, internally and artificially . . . the poem is obscure and that only one eighth of it is interpretable."[12] Veronica Forrest-Thomson did have an ingenious taste for good poetry, and she actually touched the essence of Prynne's poems. If she had grasped that to understand a poem does not necessarily mean to be able to "interpret" it in one or a few definite ways, she should have been confident in giving a fraction much greater than "one eighth". David Trotter once commented on "obscure" poetry while analysing Prynne's poems: "An 'obscure' poetry troubles because it presents the reader not with too little, but with too much, information. Far from being void of meaning, it contains an unusable *surplus*, presuming to communicate without, in the eyes of the reader, actually doing so. The reader finds himself trapped between the allure of this presumption and the opacity of its sense, overcome not by the absence of data, but by his inability to contrive uses for a surplus; an admission so damaging to his self-esteem it rapidly spawns any number of defensive manoeuvres."[13]

In the face of difficult poetry, there certainly should be a change of attitude towards "understanding" itself, so that one can feel confident to understand a difficult poem in an appropriate way. While reading a Prynne poem, one is advised to clear one's mind as a screen (not a flat screen like that of a TV, but of three or even four dimensions, depending on your own poetical and intellectual backgrounds) and then to throw the words into it, letting them hit, explode, or travel and change along the way. One will get all kinds of pictures, all images, all moods, all beauties, some of which are beyond language until they reach to the point of silent feeling and meditative enjoyment. Whatever you get composes the activity of your reading experience, the quality of which depends on the quality of your mind "screen" and the skills with which you throw the poetical words and sentences. One is strongly advised not to try to analyse the beauty, because the beauty often vanishes at the very moment when rationality interferes; just as life will often vanishes as a live being is to put on a operation dissection table and cut open. Traditionally, Chinese readers often read a good poem again and again, in a loud voice and by murmuring, in imagination and in meditation; in doing so they naturally enjoy the poetical beauties. And sometimes in China one may often memorise a poem one does not understand; only dozens of months or even dozens of years later to experience a sudden enlightenment and full enjoyment of the poem. Poetry is written to be read, not to be analysed. This is not to denigrate academic analysis, it is just suggesting that academics should stay away from poetics occasionally. "Whatever can be described by languages is big and rough; the rest that can only be felt by heart is small and delicate and cannot be described as big or small, rough or smooth."[14] The beauty of a Prynne poem often goes beyond language; therefore to appreciate a Prynne poem requires the reader to investigate around the language rather than the language itself.

Veronica Forrest-Thomson must be attempting the traditional Western way in interpreting 'Of Sanguine Fire', as she claimed that "It is hard task even to try to analyse these lines . . ."[15] If she had been trying to find a narrative structure or something that is often taught by a manual of poetics, she was sadly wrong, as "Prynne's poetry cannot be read with an expectation of finding narrative structures."[16] In fact, more and more people are realising that poetry can be against interpretation, which especially suits some of Prynne's poems. "The most recent revolution in contemporary taste in poetry—the revolution that has deposed Eliot and elevated Pound—represents a turning away from content in poetry in the old sense, an impatience with what made modern poetry prey to the zeal of interpreters."[17] Explorations and changes have never ceased to happen in the field of poetics. "Poetry is no longer seen as a series of conventions (prosodic, generic, rhetorical) which have been used to produce new versions of subjectivity, but as a capacity to imagine freshly and unconventionally."[18] Prynne is surely leading, if not creating, all these changes, or so to say, revolutions.

III. Prynne's Creation of a Unique Poetical Language

Prynne's poetry is undoubtedly different from any previous poetry in the English language, which is often taken as a new growth of the English language itself. "Mr Prynne did a lot of experiments to enhance the capacity of expression of English as a language."[19] In fact, poetry has always been the leading power in creating and enhancing English as a language, and the poetical diction, sentences, or even stanzas have formed a noble core of English. It is unimaginable that English could have become such a beautiful language if deprived of all its poetical elements. It is also the case of the Chinese language in which a lot of poetical sentences have become ordinary daily expressions. It is impossible for a language to grow without the constant contributions of poetry.

In the poetical sense, it is not exaggerated to say that Prynne's poetry is of an independent and unique poetical language. "'By refusing to become a readily accessible and intelligible writer,' Peter Ackroyd said of Prynne, 'he has ensured that poetry can no longer be treated as a deodorised museum of fine thoughts and fine feelings; he is creating, instead, a complete and coherent language.'"[20] Poetical language forms an essential part of a language, yet it is also comparatively an independent linguistic being, as it is often very distinct from other linguistic phenomena, especially in the case of Prynne who is always manoeuvring English words in an innovative manner. "Prynne uses words as exploratory instruments, packing them round the unspeakable in order that its contours may be defined. Language occupies the boundary between the sensible and the barely intelligible."[21] To Prynne, a word is not merely a word, but a clue that conjures up a train of historical events or contexts that have been deployed. And Prynne often puts some fresh flavour into a word, enhancing it or simply altering it altogether in his poetry.

Furthermore, as Prynne applies some linguistic or cultural elements other than English in his poetry, he is not to be considered as a poet of a single language or culture. "It is in the nature of Prynne's project—as it was in Pound's—to investigate the spectrum of available registers by creating a body of work large enough to include all kinds of languages."[22] Investigation of Prynne's Chinese poetical characteristics later on in this essay will offer one definitely strong argument for Prynne's international poetical character.

IV. Prynnist Poetry

Numerous attempts have been made to label Prynne's poetry, among which "post-Modernism" might be the most popular. "The apparent impossibility of achieving a complete reading of a Prynne poem, a reading which exhausts the poem's otherness, suggests that the poetry is postmodern in its indeterminacy, its avoidance of totality and closure."[23] However, other critics have offered Prynne another label by viewing him from another viewpoint. "Terminology that classifies literature is always inadequate, but this poetry can be called 'Neo-Modernist' or 'Late Modernist' owing to its depiction of various mental conditions interacting with language and cultural or natural elements."[24] Some people simply classify Prynne as a Modernist. "His [Prynne's] modernism appears totally genuine, not assumed after reaching a certain standpoint through critical argument but something the state of the language, as he experiences it, has imposed upon him. The lack of any of the traditional reverberations in the language he uses, the featherweight impact of even images and lines which can be seen, on reflection, as brilliantly expressive, must be accepted as the way he wants the world of his poetry to be..."[25] But there are also some doubts about it. "Modernism has occupied no central place in twentieth-century English poetry since there has been no necessity for it to do so."[26]

It is a pity that Prynne has never claimed himself as any "–ist" as Pound had ardently done. Neither has Prynne denied in public any label with which he has so far been crowned. In any case, Pynne's own acceptance or denial might not count too much in the eyes of critics so long as their labelling was based on sound arguments. Therefore, it seems that one is free to address Prynne as either a post-modernist, or a neo-modernist, or a late-modernist, or simply a modernist, or as anything that is to occur in the future. Although all the labels are slightly different, there is a unanimous agreement that Prynne belongs to a counter-culture tradition. "For all his perceived (and sometimes critically overplayed) isolation, Prynne belongs to a tradition, and is also part of a vigorous poetic and critical counter-culture."[27] Here, "culture" should be understood as a similar sense to pop-culture or other superficial cultural trends, rather than as some profound poetical traditions that Prynne certainly has largely inherited: "we see the author [Prynne] as a distinctively English poet working within a recognizably English lyric tradition."[28] "In the tradition" does not necessarily means to "copy the tradition", especially in the case of Prynne who inherits mainly so as to enhance and innovate.

The way to classify a poet is not an easy task, yet it is certainly an easy way to assist understandings and memories, which, nevertheless, reflects an incapability of seeing an individual poet as one without any distortion. The normal way of defining one poet is to distinguish his difference from the others, which often causes distortion. In just the same way a simile that is always helpful for memorising is always also misleading, as one is likely to see one thing in confusion with another. If one has to have similes, one should at least always remind oneself of the danger of being misled.

When one reads Prynne's poems, it is actually unnecessary, not to say impossible, to refer to other poetical works, as all possible quotations from or adoptions of the other works have been assimilated into an organic part of his poems, which stand by themselves. One can just read and enjoy this in whatever way one likes without worrying about the meaning of the "original", which constitutes an essential difference between Pound and Prynne whose work "will guide us within rather than outside itself", as discussed at the beginning of this essay. "The justification for a poetry in which metaphor seems to work without reference beyond itself and where the language exists only in itself as a self-contained system of scepticism towards whatever it has traditionally related, is that the poem will unfold itself in some form within the reader's head if brooded upon."[29] Prynne has suggested that each word is a history for him, but we do not need to trace the history of every word as Prynne has done before cooking a poem. What a reader needs to do it to enjoy, not to go to the kitchen to see what Prynne has done, and not necessarily to have the abstruse knowledge or skills that Prynne has acquired.

If the attempt at labelling Prynne causes too much trouble and confusion and too little benefit and clarification, it may be advisable simply to view Prynne as Prynne, Prynne's poetry as the work of a Prynnist poet, if an "-ist" has to be invented. "Here, Barthes touches upon the beauty of that which is '*exempt from meaning*' and upon the concept of 'beauty' itself, which is inexplicable, since 'in each part of the body it stands out, repeats itself, but it does not describe itself. Like a god (and as empty), it can only say: *I am what I am.*' These ideas about literature suit Prynne's literary objectives well . . ."[30] Prynne is Prynne, an individual who composes poems in his individual way, who is single-handedly working his way to his own ideal, which may easily make one think of the present poetical situation in China. "In contrast to his eminent position in academia, the hiddenness of Prynne's poetic career has enabled the development of an original aesthetic over three decades, a writing which runs absolutely counter to the prevailing modes of Britain and (to some extent) American poetry (though Europe and now China may offer some closer analogies)."[31] Prynne indeed shares a lot of similarities with some contemporary Chinese poets, especially some New Chinese Poets in the 1990s who insist on "Individual Creation".

V. Prynne's Connection with Chinese Poetics

Prynne was born in the 1930s when Chinese poetics had been very well studied and popularised by some Western sinologists and Modernists such as Pound and others. Thus it is inferable that Prynne must have recognised some Chinese poetical elements almost at the very moment that he cast his first eye on modernist poetry. Prynne began his formal exploration into Chinese poetics at a very early stage, which can be judged by his comment on Anne Birrell's translation of Chinese poetry. Before Prynne's serious study on the Chinese language itself, he had already read widely in English about Chinese poetry, paintings, calligraphy, music, history, science, politics etc. Prynne well understands that Chinese traditional music, painting and calligraphy are considered as inseparable from Chinese classical poetry. Prynne knows Chinese music so well and he once sponsored a piece of Daoist music for the funeral of Professor Joseph Needham, the greatest sinologist in Western history, on June 10, 1995. And Prynne's knowledge of Chinese painting is also attested by his comments on Willem de Kooning's paintings, in which Prynne applied some very professional classic Chinese painting terms.[32]

With the passage of time, Prynne, with the help of a Chinese teacher, began to practise his Mandarin, calligraphy, etc. Then, in 1986, Prynne made his first visit to China; and in 1991, he served as an English teacher for six months in Suzhou University in Jiangsu province, a place that has nurtured many great Chinese literary giants, in the past and at present. There he made many Chinese friends, with students, teachers, and people from many walks of life, and won their respect and affection. There Prynne also made friends with a group of

Chinese "Language" poets whose works Prynne arranged to introduce to Western readers; and one of them, Che Qianzi(车前子), is warmly welcomed by some Western poets, critics and readers as well.

Thus it is no wonder that Prynne's poems probe into a sphere beyond the normal reading and understanding of an English poem, pushing the art of poetry beyond the mono-cultural tradition of composing and understanding. His poetry unites the powers of English as an analytic language, and Chinese as a synthetic language. "Prynne's interest in Chinese culture places him in the line of emulators of Modernists such as Pound, Wallace Stevens, Williams, and Amy Lowell. It implies a conscious or subconscious reaction against Western *mores* in reaching out for a culture that in spite of dramatic modernisations keeps its ancient tradition alive."[33]

As Prynne assimilates everything into his "own", it is often hard if not impossible to find absolute "evidences" of his influence from Chinese poetics. We have to take more roundabout ways in this pursuit. However, one general conclusion can be drawn even before going into details: Prynne is surely influenced by Chinese poetics, considering his poetical relationship with the Western modernists and his personal involvement with China. Some Western critics have also noticed this: "From the late 1980s Prynne opened another range of reference as he explored classical and contemporary Chinese literature; there will surely be other developments too."[34] It is a pity that this statement has missed Prynne's interest in Chinese poetry before the 1980s that serves as a preparation before his later serious "leap" into China. Actually, even in the early 1960s, Prynne had co-operated with Dr. Picken and assisted with the translation of some Chinese poems for his research publication, such as the one titled as "Rainbow-skirt".[35] There are other more academic discussions on Prynne's Chinese characters: "In a wider sense, Prynne's apparent interest in conventions of Chinese poetry is a backdrop to some prominent characteristics in his writing. His own words indicate this in 'China Figures', a postscript that discusses an anthology of early Chinese love poetry in translation."[36] Prynne's Chinese poetical characteristic is surely an important and interesting element in his poetry.

Pound "moved from thing to process", notably from Imagism to Vorticism after he understood more of Chinese poetics. And in

Prynne's poetry, one can also see that the same "process" contributes a key character of Prynne's poetics. For example, as David Trotter analyses Prynne's *Brass*, he declared: ". . . I want to consider the language of *Brass* as a process of communication, rather than to provide a key to its mythologies . . ."[37] Others repeated the same experience as they read more of Prynnist poetry: "The poems are, in a sense, photographs of processes of thought, catching the instant on the wing and flying with it."[38] It is not clear how Prynne decided to compose poems in this manner, he might have even done it subconsciously, but it certainly makes one think of Chinese poetics while reading his poetry. And some critics have also noticed the "open form" of Prynne's poetry. "Granted, many of these poets [including Prynne] write 'open-ended' stanzas and poems or other 'open' forms where lines or stanzas move around the page in expressive ways."[39] The world is itself a process without an end, which is certainly what the open form of a poem or a stanza is talking about. And traditional Chinese poetics value highly the "aftertaste" and often do not want a closed end.

However, it is not suggested that Prynne made any "copy" from anyone. As Prynnist poetry declares the independence of each of its poetic element by establishing a self-referring system, the process in his poetry suddenly speeds up and obtains great power and beauty. "Prynne's poem does not rise to direct statement, or to a condemnation in Johnsonian manner of the 'great wish for calm'. By concluding precisely where it started it commits the reader to re-reading, to a further examination of the doubts sown by its internal dissensions, an *Unendlichsprechung*. Since he is never furnished with proof or exhortation, he must make his own meaning, and the effort to distinguish between the redeeming and the indulgent or schizophrenic versions of self-estrangement is a necessary part of the process."[40] Traditionally, people often compare prose as "walking" and poetry as "dancing": "The distinction is illustrated and enforced by analogies between prose and walking in the one hand, and between poetry and dancing on the other."[41] But as one reads a Prynnist poem, one feels like flying, not "as a cloud" but as by jet. "The poems [of Prynne] are, in a sense, photographs of processes of thought, catching the instant on the wing and flying with it."[42] Take a passage from Prynne's *Pearls That Were* as an example:

Slick film so crested in white reward
    its part look, part tamper
by stilted welcome to burnish its side
    at a blush, in singled halter.

Yellow on black mineral for a twitter
    bar to wing, flight to span up
snowblink through lime glass appearing,
    must not be loaded hot.

Let in the water, dazzled in their eyes,
    aroused to cry at either turn
or fledge past the slipper line of days
    that run, that are so soon.

Siskin in flocks, arab takeaway larder
    won't despise what can't be told:
tie fast to fix up a ragged flag, further
    for brokered news, new for old.

No one with a good imagination can fail to feel the speedy shifts
from one image to another, from one action to another, from one
perspective to another, from one mood to another ... A couple of lines
seem to be containing the happenings of a few centuries condensed.
As one finishes the whole sequence of *Pearls That Were*, one might feel
that one is not reading a not-too-long poem, but a whole history of
Lyricism that has developed for thousands of years as well as unlimited
expectations of its future. All diction in *Pearls That Were* is so exact,
concise and imaginative that it certainly outdoes Pound and many
other poets in the English language; each word in the poem is like
a pearl, shining radiantly and by sound, and together they form an
historic symphony as well as a poetical light that runs throughout the
past, the present and the future. Eliot's famous "objective correlative"
can also find trace here, "The only way of expressing emotion in the
form of art is by finding an 'objective correlative'; in other words,
a set of objects, a situation, a chain of events which shall be the
formula of that particular emotion; such that when the external facts,

which must terminate in sensory experience, are given, the emotion is immediately evoked."[43] In Prynne's *Pearls That Were*, one finds no outspoken emotional diction while feeling very strong emotion in every single line huddled with "objectives".

Undoubtedly, Prynne's diction fits well with the way that a traditional Chinese poet would compose his poetry. "On the whole, Prynne's sententious poetic diction shares a number of significant characteristics with Oriental poetry. This is obvious in ontological impressions, precision, brevity, and syntactic or thematic minimalism. The dynamics of the visual form in his poems, furthermore, display characteristics that can be traced back via Pound and Olson to Chinese and Japanese poetic forms."[44] And the poetical sentences composed by Prynne's diction also provoke the imagination of many Chinese scenes, even in some Western readers' minds. In *Nearly Too Much: The Poetry of J.H. Prynne* we find: "All the components of this 'cycle' feature prominently in *The Oval Window*, as does the idea of a cycle itself (pp.13, 16, 17 ['recycle'], 18, 28 ['cyclical']). The recurrent motif of the 'screen' in particular sets up a bizarre link between the distant cultures, as the intricately-decorated Chinese folding screens and the video display units can both be used as surrogates for the otherwise inaccessible world that is represented on them:

> ...
> ...
>
> Drawn to the window and beyond it,
> By the heartfelt screen of a machine
> tenderly lit sideways
>
> (p.30)

In this last example, the Chinese screen could be 'heartfelt'... —from the emotional charge carried—and in a sense carried away—by its symbolic landscape paintings."[45]

Unlike Pound who applied Chinese characters directly in his *Cantos*, Prynne assimilates Chinese poetics into his poetry and makes it an organic part of his method, harmonising it with all the other poetical elements. In the poem *The Oval Window*, Prynne widely borrowed from Chinese poetical elements from the book of Chinese poetry *Among the Flowers*.[46] Prynne borrowed some sentences from this book, such as "As they parted, she heard his horse cry out" (*Among the Flowers*, p.38), "brushed / in azure along the folding screen." (*Among the Flowers*, p.87), "Her wrists shine white like the frosted snow." (*Among the Flowers*, p.60), and dozens of others. Besides, in *The Oval Window* Prynne also adapted many poetical phrases and diction from *Among the Flowers*. For example, if one compares the two lines in *The Oval Window* "a mist of gold leaf lightly shimmers / as flowers clouds go back to the mountains" with the lines in *Among the Flowers* "The mountains on the screen shimmer in the golden dawn / A cloud of hair brushes the fragrant snow of her cheek" (p.37.), one would see the relationship very definitely. In fact, as one reads and compares the two works of *The Oval Window* and *Among the Flowers*, one cannot help thinking that the former being a crystallised and Prynnised version of the latter.

With such a wide range of poetical elements in Prynne's poetry, it is natural that many a reader may feel the effect to be colourful, yet strange or even bizarre as well. "In Prynne's poems we find metamorphoses, spectacular and menacing natural phenomena, man-made disasters and cosmic ructions tapering down to the 'home world'; but also, and infrequently mentioned, a fine ear for rhythm and cadence, and a way of managing lyric in strange and dazzling ways."[47] And another "strange" character of Prynne the poet himself is that he composes much more than he comments. "Unlike other poets who also lecture, Prynne has published very little academic criticism or scholarship and he has maintained a distance from the metropolitan literary scene. He has however been a mentor and influence for many writers through his practice and wide correspondence."[48] During the Modernist period, poets such as Pound and Eliot did write a lot about poetics, even more than their poems. "He [Philip Larkin] has surrounded the approach to his poems with complaints that academics and students destroy the relationship between literature and life. 'Poetry has lost its old audience,' he said in 1957, two years after the publication of *The Less Deceived*. 'This has been caused by the consequences of a cunning merger between poet, literary critic and academic critic (three classes now notoriously indistinguishable).'"[49] However, Prynne's behaviour is very much different from them while very similar to some Tang Dynasty Chinese poets: "It is said that the Tang Dynasty poets did not know much poetics, but they composed magnificent poems; however, the Song Dynasty poets talked a lot about poetics, but they wrote only few good poems."[50] Prynne has certainly read widely and known a lot about poetics, both traditional and modern, although he did not write many essays. Prynne seems to be insisting that a poet should speak BY his work, not FOR his work.

If the above arguments about Prynne's Chinese poetical characteristics are only "traces", the poem that Prynne composed in Chinese is certainly a hard proof for Prynne's involvement with Chinese poetics. In Prynne's Chinese poem "Jieban Mi Shihu ('结伴觅石湖'), which he published in his own Chinese calligraphy—a traditional Chinese way—Prynne well demonstrates his overall scholarship of Chinese poetics. Ezra Pound had also been fascinated about Chinese poetry and Chinese culture, yet he was never able to come to China himself, not to say to compose anything in Chinese language. Thus it is appropriate to conclude that Chinese poetics is continuously deepening its influence on the Western poetical circle until now.

Notes

[1] Veronica Forrest-Thomson, *Poetic Artifice: A Theory of Twentieth-Century Poetry* (Manchester: Manchester University Press, 1978) p.142.

[2] Robert Potts, 'Through the Oval Window', *The Guardian*, April 4, 2004. p.36. The translator of 'Pearls That Were' is the author of this essay. The Chinese translation of 'Pearls That Were' was published in the sixth issue of *World Literature* in 2005, the first journal in PR. China dedicated to introducing and studying foreign literature. The journal is widely circulated in China, but the exact number of each issue sold is difficult to tell, as it might vary from thousands to tens of thousands.

[3] N.H. Reeve and Richard Kerridge, *Nearly Too Much: The Poetry of J.H. Prynne* (Liverpool: Liverpool University Press, 1995) p.vii (Preface).

[4] Roger Caldwell, 'The flight back to where we are', review of J.H. Prynne, *Poems* (South Fremantle and Newcastle upon Tyne, 1999—henceforward *Poems* 1999), *TLS*, 5012 (April 23, 1999) p. 27.

[5] Alan Halsey, 'Prynne Collected', review of J.H. Prynne, *Poems* (Edinburgh

and London, 1982—henceforward *Poems* 1982), *PN Review*, 31 (Vol. 9 No. 5) (1983), 76–79. p.77.

6 *Nearly Too Much*, p. 182.

7 Anne Birrell, *New Songs from a Jade Terrace* (Harmondsworth: Penguin Books, 1986) p.391.

8 *Contemporary British Poetry: Essays in Theory and Criticism,* ed. James Acheson and Romana Huk (New York: State University of New York Press, 1996) p.14. (Introduction, by Romana Huk).

9 Dennis Keene, 'In Extenso', review of, *int. al.*, *Poems* 1982, *PN Review*, 30 (Vol. 9 No. 4) (1982), 63–67. p. 64.

10 Nigel Wheale, 'The Crossing Flow of Even Life', review of J.H. Prynne, *Poems. Tarset,* Bloodaxe Books, 1999, *Stand*, 4 (1999), 75–8. p.77.

11 T.S. Eliot, 'The Metaphysical Poets' (pp. 281–291.), *Selected Essays* (London: Faber and Faber, 1954) p.289.

12 Veronica Forrest-Thomson, *Poetic Artifice,* p.48

13 David Trotter, 'A Reading of Prynne's *Brass*', *PN Review*, 6 (Vol. 5 No. 2) (1977), 49–53, p.49.

14 Chen Guying, *Introduction to Zhuangzi* (Beijing: Sanlian Bookshop, 1998) p.60.

15 *Poetic Artifice*, p.144.

16 Birgitta Johansson, *The Engineering of Being: An Ontological Approach to J.H. Prynne* (Uppsala: Swedish Science Press, 1997) p.19.

17 Susan Sontag, 'Against Interpretation', David Lodge, *20th Century Literary Criticism* (London: Longman Group Limited, 1972) p.658.

18 David Trotter, *The Making of the Reader: Language and Subjectivity in Modern American, English and Irish Poetry* (London: Macmillan Press, 1984) p.243.

19 *Nearly Too Much*, p. 1.

20 *The Making of the Reader*, p. 242.

21 Elizabeth Cook, 'Prynne's Principia', review of *Poems* 1982, *London Review of Books,* Vol. 4 No. 17 (16 September–6 October 1982), 15–16. p.16.

22 Jeremy Noel-Tod, 'A Bird that Isn't There', *London Review of Books*, February 8, 2001, p.33.

23 *Nearly Too Much*, p.2.

24 *The Engineering of Being*, p.5.

25 'In Extenso', p.65.

26 'In Extenso', p.65.

27 Patrick McGuinness, 'Going Electric', *London Review of Books,* Vol. 22 No. 17 (7 September, 2000), pp.31–32. p.31.

28 Alan Halsey, 'Prynne Collected', review of *Poems* 1982, *PN Review*, 31

(Vol. 9 No. 5) (1983), 76–79. p.77.

[29] 'In Extenso', p.64.

[30] *The Engineering of Being*, p.14.

[31] 'The Crossing Flow of Even Life', p.76.

[32] J.H. Prynne, 'A Discourse on Willem de Kooning's Rosy-Fingered Dawn at Louse Point', *act 2, art, criticism and theory* (London,1996), pp.34–73.

[33] *The Engineering of Being*, p.187.

[34] 'The Crossing Flow of Even Life', p.78.

[35] L. E. R. Picken, "Secular Chinese Songs of the Twelfth Century" (pp.125–172*), Studia Musicologica Academiae Scientiarum Hungaricae*, 8, 1966. pp.144–145; compare Prynne's more free and "orientalised" reworking of Picken's literal translation, published in *Collection*, 1 (March, 1968); pp. 43–44.

[36] *The Engineering of Being*, p.192.

[37] 'A Reading of Prynne's *Brass*', p.49.

[38] Ian Patterson, ' "the medium itself, rabbit by proxy": some thoughts about reading J.H. Prynne'; *Poets on Writing: Britain, 1970–1991*, ed. Denise Riley (London: Macmillan, 1992) p.234.

[39] Edward Larrissy, 'Poets of *A Various Art*: J.H. Prynne'; Veronica Forrest-Thomson, Andrew Crozier *Contemporary British Poetry*, p.63.

[40] 'A Reading of Prynne's *Brass*', p.52.

[41] Paul Valéry, 'Poetry and Abstract Thought: Dancing and Walking'; David Lodge, *20th Century Literary Criticism.* (London: Longman, 1972.) p.253.

[42] *Poets on Writing*, p.234.

[43] 'Hamlet', *Selected Essays,* p.145.

[44] *The Engineering of Being*, pp. 187–188.

[45] *Nearly Too Much*, pp.180–181.

[46] *Among the Flowers: the Hua-chien chi*, comp. by Chao Ch'ung-tso, trans. by Lois Fusek (New York: Columbia University Press, 1982).

[47] 'Going Electric', p.31.

[48] 'The Crossing Flow of Even Life', p.76.

[49] Andrew Motion, *Philip Larkin* (London: Methuen, 1982) p.11.

[50] Guo Shaoyu, *A History of Chinese Criticism* (I, II) (Tianjing: Baihua Literature and Art Publishing House, 1999) p.329.

'A FREE HAND TO REFUSE EVERYTHING': POLITICS AND INTRICACY IN THE WORK OF J.H. PRYNNE

Rod Mengham

For over thirty years, from 1968 to 1999, Prynne's poetry was written and published within a context of networks of distribution and reception which were not the economic networks available to, or employed by, poets with a more conventional, more easily assimilable, poetic. His work was framed by the avant-garde activity of journals such as *The English Intelligencer* and *The Grosseteste Review* and by small presses such as Cape Goliard, Trigram, Ferry Press, Street Editions, Equipage and Barque. Poets operating within this circuit could rely on their audience having in some degree the status of interlocutors; they were not writing without knowing to whom they were speaking; neither were the readers they were addressing being construed as reflections of a universal subject. At the same time, the experimental nature of their work on language extended what might otherwise seem the very restricted scope of their activities, by holding out the possibility of constituting at some point in the future the conditions of a pragmatic situation that would not have existed before. The possibility arose, and still arises, of the work creating its own readers, in a fulfilment of the scenario outlined by Merleau-Ponty in his book *The Prose of the World*:

> The public at whom the artist aims is not given; it is a public to be elicited by his work. The others of whom he thinks are not empirical 'others' or even *humanity* conceived as a species; it is others once they have become such that he can live with them.[1]

The point about such an avant-garde poetry is that this forward projection is in tension with an awareness of the way that subjectivity is determined historically at the moment of production of the text. There is an unusually direct and declarative treatment of the urgent necessity for setting up and maintaining this tension in Prynne's poem 'L'Extase de M. Poher' from the 1971 volume, *Brass*: [2]

Why do we ask that, as if wind in the
telegraph wires were nailed up in some
kind of answer, formal derangement of
the species. Days and weeks spin by in
theatres, gardens laid out in rubbish, this
is the free hand to refuse everything.
          No
question provokes the alpha rhythm by
the tree in our sky turned over; certain
things follow:
       who is the occasion
          now   what
       is the question in
          which   she
       what for is a version
          of when, i.e.
some payment about time again and how
"can sequence conduce" to order as more
than the question: more gardens: list
       the plants as distinct
          from   lateral
       front to back or not
          grass   "the most
       successful plant on our
          heart-lung by–
pass and into passion sliced into bright
slivers, the yellow wrapping of what we do.
Who is it: what person could be generalised
on a basis of "specifically" sexual damage,
the townscape of that question.
          Weather
of the wanton elegy, take a chip out of
your right thumb. Freudian history again makes
       the thermal bank: here
          credit   92%
       a/c payee only, reduce to
          now   what

laid out in the body
            sub-normal
or grass etc, hay as a touch of the
social self put on a traffic island. Tie
that up, over for next time, otherwise there
is a kind of visual concurrence;
                        yet
the immediate body of wealth is not
history, body-fluid not dynastic. No
poetic gabble will survive which fails
to collide head-on with the unwitty circus:
            no history running
                    with the French horn into
                            the alley-way, no
                    manifest emergence
            of valued instinct, no growth
                    of meaning & stated order:
            we are too kissed & fondled,
            no longer instrumental
            to culture in "this" sense or
            any free-range system of time:
                1. Steroid metaphrast
                2. Hyper-bonding of the insect
                3. 6% memory, etc
any other rubbish is mere political rhapsody, the
gallant lyricism of the select, breasts & elbows,
                what
else is allowed by the verbal smash-up piled
under foot. Crush tread trample distinguish
put your choice in the hands of the town
clerk, the army stuffing its drum. Rubbish is
            pertinent; essential; the
            most intricate presence in
            our entire culture; the
ultimate sexual point of the whole place turned
            into a model question.

'No poetic gabble will survive which fails / to collide head-on with the unwitty circus': this seems to be a clear injunction to resume the historic avant-garde practice of forcing the work of art back into the context of social practice as a whole; no artistic project which fails to extricate itself from the cultural annexe ('the alley-way') to which the bourgeois phase of history has confined it will have any long-term or far-reaching effect. The special task of art for a bourgeois culture— the task of preserving intact the means of describing the values of instinctual life, of coherence, order and completeness—may serve as a means of prolonging the absence of these qualities from social reality. Insofar as the work of art adheres to principles of organicism and symmetry in its composition, this may allow it to become a satisfying means of compensation for what would otherwise be felt as too gaping a lack in everyday life. Readers and writers in this cultural condition are 'too kissed & fondled', too beguiled by the status accorded to art as a form of discourse that has been mystified, regarded as something superior to, aloof from, those apparently less valuable discursive practices which register the laws and operations of existing moral and political forms and social arrangements. The flattery lavished on 'high' art is what deprives it of its social function, so that it is 'no longer instrumental / to culture in "this" sense': the inverted commas around the word 'this' serve ironically as an allusion to the bracketed state of art, its no more than parenthetical presence in the culture as a whole. The poem 'L'Extase de M. Poher' provides a counter-example to this in its opening with inverted commas of a quotation that is never allowed to terminate. What appears to be the isolation and placing of a fragment of scientific discourse—'the most / successful plant on our / heart-lung by- / pass'—passes rapidly but imperceptibly into a head-on collision with an obviously experimental poetic diction that completely unsettles the register: 'and into passion sliced into bright / slivers, the yellow wrapping of what we do'. Here we have an almost hyperbolically systematic application of the basic avant-garde principle of montage, which undermines the sequential coherence of those discursive practices that would otherwise 'conduce' to the kind of social and political order that depends on the subordination, or bracketing, of discourses like poetry, because these represent the threat of a potentially much freer attitude towards the dominant syntax of history. Later on in the poem, there is a quite violent interpolation of scientific discourse, which represents a recognition within the poem of the need to measure the effects of a culturally much more powerful description of the conditions in which the subject of history has to emerge. The actual material involved—'1. Steroid metaphrast / 2. Hyper-bonding of the insect / 3. 6% memory, etc'—makes it clear that what this collision of languages and subject matters effects is the displacement of the subject of anthropological humanism; a displacement, moreover, in a particular direction and for a particular purpose. The alternative to this discursive confrontation is satirised in a ludicrous evocation of the historic avant-garde as an advance column, in marching order, not in advance of an utopian form of society to come, but heading up an entire army of philistine recuperation, 'stuffing its drum'. The apparently destructive effect of this accentuated montage, this 'verbal smash-up', destroys recognizable forms of order and coherence, produces debris, produces rubbish. But the production of rubbish is essential since it is the inevitable outcome of testing the limits of the sequential procedures of an ideologizing rationality.[3] Paradoxically, the moment when you think you are in full control of your own subjectivity is precisely when you 'put your choice in the hands of the town / clerk'. This information is given in the form of an instruction which tests the limits of the reader's own dependence on the conditions of 'stated order'. Discursive friction, then, provides a means of turning art back into an 'intricate presence in / our entire culture'; threading it back into the fabric of the whole, making it intrinsic to social practice.

Prynne's deliberate confrontation with bourgeois consumer culture in the late 1960s and early 1970s is reconfigured in subsequent work. By the late 1970s and early 1980s, when several American 'Language' poets were formulating the nature of their desire to subvert capitalist culture by textual means, Prynne had already overtaken this formalism on the route to a different model. By the mid-1980s, several 'Language' writers had issued theoretical bulletins recommending the production of poetry in which capitalist procedures of accumulation were deranged by a methodical squandering of meaning; hoarding replaced by spending. Prynne seized on the economic vocabulary ('the market-economy model seems to me to fit the case very well'[4]) to argue that the resulting 'freedom' of choice among the potential meanings offered to the reader was no more than cosmetic:

> if it is at all accepted that distributive justice cannot adequately be modelled on a plan of competitive demand management with added cosmetic 'choice', then the cosmetics of choice become the most dangerous elements: they destroy vigilance and all sense of an interconnected general good by seeming to provide a rewarding increase in benefits for those defined as deserving (earning) (acquiring) them.[5]

The illusory liberations of 'Language' poetry did little more than force the reader to respond to conventional pressures of meaning not by diverting their force into genuinely new channels but simply by letting them peter out. No attempt was made to explore other possibilities implicit in the scope of the 'central' analogy between grammatical and narrative structures on the one hand and the profit structures of capitalism on the other; no consideration was given to the prospect that if the linear perspective of political economy is such a devastating model for thinking about language, that does not prevent a review of separate orders of transaction.

This is precisely what Prynne's *Word Order* (1989) does provide in its intricate examination of the way in which particular examples of language-use, or 'word orders', bear within them the history of the development of social forms; in particular, they show how the societies of the west are governed by a particular kind of order, the economic order. The language of this poem is repeatedly focussed in a comparison between the kinds of word order that are enforced or commanded—ordered—by a capitalist economy and the possibilities broached by quite different kinds of word order that could be related to entirely different types of economies, specifically, gift economies of the kind researched by Marcel Mauss in his seminal book *The Gift*.[6]

Mauss describes a number of societies in which money does not exist, but where an economy is established through the perpetual transfer of gifts; members of these societies give to others whatever their wealth consists in—land, food, labour, for instance—and receive from others whatever they need, also in the form of gifts. The gift will not be responded to immediately and may never be responded to in kind (a gift of food may elicit a donation of labour). The obligation incurred by the receipt of the gift is difficult if not impossible to quantify, which means that the bond established between givers and receivers is both more personal and is maintained on a more universal basis than in many economies. In this context, words like 'give' and 'take' are under a great deal of semantic pressure:

> We inserted our names would we sing
>   out on sight and give in full
> the free the offer repeatedly, hit as he lay on
>   the ground stroked no struck to put
> words into the mouth the truth the life
>   and take the ethereal vapour
>   like a chance
> crossing the street.[7]

'Giving' and 'taking' mean very different things in the context of a capitalist economy. The colloquial phrase 'give and take' is habitually used in a spirit of reciprocity—it starts to reconcile terms that are normally marked for disagreement, although it still does not sink the obvious differences between them. In a gift economy, the activity of giving would be regarded as very much the same sort of transaction as the activity of taking. In certain gift economies, according to Mauss, it is possible for 'only a single word to cover [what we understand by] buy and sell, borrow and lend'[8]; seemingly antithetical operations are expressed by exactly the same word. A whole variety of exchanges— of food, marriage partners, possessions, charms, land, labour, services, religious offices (nearly all alluded to in *Word Order*)—are not seen as being discrete; what would be thought of as heterogeneous social phenomena in the West are regarded as part of the same economy, the same order of meaning. According to Mauss, 'each phenomenon contains all the threads of which the social fabric is composed'[9]; this now seems a strange idea in a capitalist society, but it is precisely what Prynne tries to make the intrinsic method for producing his text: each

verbal phenomenon contains many, if not all, of the threads of which
the whole fabric of the text is composed. This vocabulary of threads
and fabrics is reminiscent of Barry MacSweeney's *Wild Knitting* and
of the project of 'L'Extase de M.Poher', aimed at turning art back into
an 'intricate presence in / our entire culture'—threading it back into
the fabric of the whole, making it intrinsic to social practice.

In *Word Order*, contemporary Western society is disclosed as not
operating in terms of this kind of social fabric; its coherence is seen
rather as that of a textured surface, where certain meanings are fused
together in word orders that are dictated by a ruthless economy of
exchange, one in which 'the capital is reported to be quiet'.[10] This
phrase suggests that the capital city is reported to be quiet, but also that
financial capital is reckoned to be quiet; it is the kind of formulation
that issues from a bureau of official statements, one whose placations
actually betray an underlying unrest. The role of the poem is to act
on this restiveness, this underlying unrest, in order to stop the trade
of 'value for money'[11] and show how the language of profit and loss
is caught up in the inflicting of damage in ways that are normally *not*
reported. In this poem, a phrase like 'take a cut'[12] comprises a sense
of taking a share of the proceeds but only alongside something else; it
also becomes part of a vivid but almost subliminal account of personal
injury. The writing is concerned to undo phrases like this—it undoes
a whole series of language-constructs, following, as it were, the path
of the gift.

I put it this way, because one of the main points about keeping gifts
in circulation without changing them into money is that they then
behave in some measure, as Mauss puts it, like 'parts of the persons'
involved in their interchange; the passing and repassing of gifts sets up
a pattern of spiritual bonds, a perpetual transfer of 'spiritual matter'.[13]
Some of the most important word orders have been established with
reference to the operations of spirit (and in this poem there is actually
a register associating 'spirit' with 'purity' and 'truth'); these are word
orders that have often been achieved by means of incantation, ritual
and the maintenance of very powerful conventions. The languages
of spiritual values are in fact what secular power needs to fill with
its own business: to 'put / words into the mouth the truth the life'
is to replace the notion of speech as divine gift ('I am the truth and

the life') with a pragmatics of control ('put / words into the mouth') that requires all the usual connections between 'truth' and 'life' to be remade.

According to Mauss, the forms of communicating with spirit are, for gift societies, the most important to develop, the most risky, the most dangerous to omit: 'the first groups of beings with whom men must have made contracts were the spirits of the dead and the gods. They in fact are the real owners of the world's wealth.'[14]

Contracts with the dead, in which proprietorship is an issue, and rights are reciprocal if not exactly symmetrical, can be maintained through linguistic conventions and literary forms; though the relation of these contracts to presiding values and usages in contemporary western societies is subject to progressive displacement by more and more 'spiritless forms': 'would we sing / out on sight and give in full / the free the offer'; the separation of terms usually made indistinguishable by cliché ('the free the offer', rather than 'free offer') restores an element of quality to what has been absorbed into calculations of quantity. The requirement to 'give in full' vulgarises 'giving' as the obligation to state a 'fullness' that is actually no more than a minimal projection of self. (When you give your name in full, how much of yourself do you really give?) In its first line, the poem registers the deformed capacity of song ('would we sing / out on sight'), and its devalued vocabulary of 'freedom', 'gift' and 'offer' provides a revision of song as no more than 'compliance'—as it says on p.373—with a pneumatic fake, raising 'wind *as* with one voice' (my emphasis): going through a pretence of unison or wholeness. Much of the language of the poem is pinched or bruised by officialese; the first line begins by appearing to fill in a form—'We inserted our names'—and from that point on come what seem like occasional responses to a questionnaire; at one point, the reader is instructed to 'answer each question'.[15]

Congress with the dead, maintaining a contract with the spirits of the dead, appears at certain points in the poem to have become warped into supplying details for a report on an accident victim. The tones of the poem tend to revolve around an axis that goes from elegy to inquest or 'enquiry'[16]; the tiny splinters of social scenery glimpsed in the writing from time to time reflect two scenarios in the main: a traffic smash-up and a 'burying ground'. It is highly significant that several intimations of death are focussed on a kind of limbo state; on the condition of the body while it is in the middle of a physiological reaction. What the writing is constantly wondering about is what happens to flesh when it is contunded, what happens to brains when they are concussed, and, most especially, what happens in the process of the most important of all forms of 'giving' and 'taking, the giving and taking of breath? The 'auscultation' referred to on the last page is both clinical and divinatory; a divination of spirits and the operation of listening to hear whether and how the patient is still breathing. The lapse of attention that accompanies the indrawing of breath is what gives order to words by establishing a measure (the 'frame' is 'clipped' by 'lapse indrawn'[17]). The taking of breath is posited as a form of bracing or protection, while song is construed as the giving of a cry after the blow has been struck in order to report on what has been endured. What comes between these two moments—of taking and giving—when nothing much can be said, is a lapse, a surcease. It seems commensurate with this, that the poem is particularly interested in the use of the particles 'ah' and 'O', and it isn't merely coincidental that the writing of *Word Order* dates from the same time as Prynne's British Academy lecture of 10 November 1988, 'English Poetry and Emphatical Language'[18], which is concerned especially with the use of the word 'O' in English poetry.

The struggle for breath, then, is the basis of form, and in this respect the elaborate artifice of poetry comes closer than any other art form to questions of sheer survival. In the contemporary social fabric—or rather, textured surface—this craft of necessity is judged as no more than an amenity that is rateable on the leisure scale: the 'rush for breath' gets transformed into 'taking the air', the emergency that occurs 'in no time', is recovered from in no time 'at all.'[19]

The history of literary form may go in one of two ways: it may develop a long intimacy with the moment of loss and perturbation that supplies order, or it may pull back to a safe distance from that through repeated touches at the unfeeling scars in the hardened language of a restrictive word order. The crucial fractions of time in the process are spatialized in manoeuvres of 'standing back' from and 'standing clear'[20] of the event, of the lapse of attention, the lapse of consciousness, that can only be written about, spoken of, sung; can only be refigured once it can be numbly sequenced: 'before avoid returning.'[21] The distance brings reassurance, power, and amasses other kinds of stock. The subject constructed by an economy based on private property, the private self, is seen as vengefully impoverished: 'In the wash-house / we saw their faces we gathered up / our belongings, we heard them and it was / not in this word order, cannot be afraid.'[22] The use of parataxis, in a succession of clauses without connectives, is only succeeded by connection and control with the introduction of an impersonal construction: 'and it was / not in this word order.' It makes an authentic language of personal agency sound almost impossible of achievement. The retractedness of much of the writing stems from this near-impossibility of establishing genuine word orders, when the kinds of regulation the writing tries constantly to verge on are constantly assailed by the brutal and contradictory demands of a language of profit and loss. It could hardly be otherwise in a capitalist society where discrete social phenomena have developed inner logics of their own, although the poem constantly insists on the parallels that exist between them and searches also for some principle or principles that would govern this parallelism. The connection between literary, linguistic and other kinds of order—social, political and economic— seems to me to be addressed in the last few lines of the poem in their recognizing the problem of a form that may go on (on and on in history) but which also goes *through*: weaving through and through its own material 'all the threads of which the social fabric is composed':

> . . . had you not better
> with a metal spike the axis
> of ah, attention, no liquid, frame clipped
> by lapse indrawn and hit
> in no time or at all there is
> exactly to the front of this
> on the paper hoop as a form
> goes on through.[23]

Word Order provides an effective modelling of the activity proposed in

'L'Extase de M.Poher' as a means of turning art back into an 'intricate presence in / our entire culture.' Its imaginative grasp of the scope of gift economies is focussed on the behaviour of what Mauss refers to 'archaic societies'. *News of Warring Clans* (1977) had negotiated a parallel relationship with archaic forms of nomadism. In the texts published during the 1990s and since, the ideological operation of the western state has been evaluated through stark juxtaposition with the forms and relations of contemporary non-Western societies, particularly of China and of the Middle East.

A decisive shift in this direction is manifest in *Not-You* (1993), separated from *Word Order* in Prynne's collected poems by the Chinese text of the poem 'Jie ban mi shi hu.' In its dedication to Chinese poets, in its allusion to sixteenth century Indian painting ('peacock in a rainstorm at night') and in its citation of Michael Donhauser, the Lichtensteinian poet who has experimented with Japanese verse forms, *Not-You* puts down several powerful markers for the significance of Prynne's increasing interest in a kind of reverse orientalism, in the performance of elective affinities amounting almost to a disavowal of inherited cultural relations. At the same time, the opening reference to twins and recurrent glimpses of domestic antagonism introduce the circumscription of genetic links and familiarised connections. Generic intimacy, ideologically sanctioned, is evoked precisely through instances of its failure, its reliance on surrogate forms of the discourse it is meant to embody: 'Her hymnal by the bed, his sheltered / housing'[24]. Across the sequence, there is almost a narrative of simultaneous coupling and uncoupling, with masculine and feminine pronouns swerving away from mutuality. The singularity of self is made to seem irremediable through linguistic replication; predicates do not extend the self into the world but suggest its infinite capacity for self-reflection: '*she shielded, he heating . . . We* do *weld*' (my emphases). That last verb is a typical recruit to the governing tension of a need to suture, or repair, various kinds of division: 'We do weld, the / seam holding sun flakes scatters dis- / cussion forward only roused'[25]. Technically, the poem 'shakes apart' [*dis-quatere*] that which its language holds together, and the enjambement provides a simple demonstration of its ability to enforce slanting links between elements that a linear reading would seem to break apart. In the longest poem of the sequence, resistance to horizontality arises from and consolidates a form of 'trust': 'a rising vertical trust: enough to clear / line to line clasp essentials'[26]. The enjambement also acts as a reminder of the writing's unusual predilection for hyphenated phrases, the point being that you can hyphenate anything; create meaning through relations where none existed previously. The hyphenated title speaks of the necessity for this to be more than self-seeding; of the necessity for joining the self with what it is not.

The separateness of what is joined is a blighted condition arousing expectations of a need for treatment, specifically for 'cure', although 'cure' is labelled 'terrible' on one page that counterpoints it with 'care'[27]. The final appearance of the word—'air's cure'—converts it from remedy to a means of arresting decay, when accelerated decomposition might be preferable: 'No acts / rot more slowly in the memory'[28]. The penultimate page in the sequence instructs the reader to 'Condemn this song . . . to lie down; not yet rising / star now clean slain to spare either'[29]. Between the alternatives of mercy and condemnation, the focal role is that of 'rising' trust, by means of which language hyphenates—both joins and separates—identical and non-identical elements. 'Clean' and 'slain' are not only half rhymes, they also recall the separation of Western and Eastern branches of the Indo-European family of languages according to the *centum/satem* test, dividing languages into those which begin their word for a hundred with a 'k' sound, and those which use an 's' sound.

A lack of trust is identified with the absence of certain kinds of reading, 'causing the forest / to fail softly by watching leaves turn.'[30]. Organic decay is shadowed by the turning pages of a book; the double meaning is there in English, but is even stronger in Italian, whose 'foglia / foglio' is premeditated in the slight vertical pressure exerted on the verb 'fail'. The action of trust in the world, highlighted in the epigraph taken from David Lewis, requires a practice of language which is not simply described in poetry, but which in its meshing of identical and non-identical elements is ineradicably poetic. 'Trust' and 'care' are what distinguish the work of poetry from the operations of a western economy that 'destroy vigilance and all sense of an interconnected general good'[31].

NOTES

1. Maurice Merleau-Ponty, *The Prose of the World* (London: Heinemann, 1974), p.86

2. J.H. Prynne, *Poems* (Tarset: Bloodaxe Books, 2005) pp.161–2

3. Prynne's most recently published sequence is entitled 'Refuse Collection', in *in blossoms atop reeds it flares*, anthology edited by Chris Brownsword (Broken Compass Press, 2006) pp.16–19

4. J.H. Prynne, 'Letter to Ashley Hayles', *The Language Issue*, Number 1, (1992); reprinted as 'Letter to Steve McCaffery' in *The Gig*, No.7, ed Nate Dorward (November, 2000); the text of this letter was sent originally to Steve McCaffery on 2 January 1989.

5. Ibid

6. Marcel Mauss, *The Gift: Forms and Functions of Exchange in Archaic Societies*, trans. Ian Cunnison (London: Cohen and Weir, 1954).

7. *Poems*, p.360

8. Mauss, p.30

9. Ibid, p.1

10. *Poems*, p.360

11. Ibid, p.373

12. Ibid, p.363

13. Mauss, p.12

14. Mauss, p.13

15. Poems, p.371

16. Ibid, p.371

17. Ibid, p.377

18. *Proceedings of the British Academy*, Vol. LXXIV (1988) pp.135-169

19. *Poems*, p.377

20. Ibid, p.372

21. Ibid

22. Ibid, p.360

23. Ibid, p.377

24. Ibid, p.406

25. Ibid

26. Ibid, p.394

27. Ibid

28. Ibid, p.407

29. Ibid

30. Ibid

31. 'Letter to Ashley Hayles'

HANGING ON YOUR EVERY WORD
J.H. Prynne's *Bands Around The Throat*
and a Dialectics of planned impurity

Simon Perril

Despite his initial debt to Olson, even Prynne's early works *Kitchen Poems* and *The White Stones* show a wilful interrogation of the speech-based "Projective verse" model. Instead, utterance is more often maimed and wounded by a self-conscious sense of inappropriateness and inadequacy. In "Concerning Quality, Again" the voice chides "I draw blood whenever I open my stupid mouth" (*Poems*, p.81), and the supposedly transitional collection *Brass*, utters perhaps the most haunting line in Prynne's oeuvre: ". . . we have already induced / moral mutation in the species" (*Poems*, p.165). However, this sense of contamination is also held in check by a suspicion of any reactionary fleeing to notions of purity. The work of the 1980's seems to constantly wrestle with issues of voice and address; not so much to abandon them as indicative of a cosy critique of "authorial presence", but to re-instate them as necessary impurities. The text of this period that seems most merciless in its scrutiny of the positioning of the poet / speaker and what such a standpoint lays claim to is the 1987 collection *Bands Around The Throat*.

Bands is notable, formally, for its return to a model of individually titled poems—a form that Prynne had not employed since at least *Vernal Aspects* and *The Land of Saint Martin*, and more obviously *Wound Response*—a form to which he would not return until *Her Weasels Wild Returning*. Two forms of meltdown constellate around this text: firstly, the nuclear accident at Chernobyl in May 1986, contaminating large areas of Western Russia, Scandinavia and northwest Europe in the first ten days alone. And secondly—though more by anticipation, as the event postdates the actual publication date—Black Monday; the collapse of the New York Stock Exchange on October 19, 1987 and the chain reaction felt throughout the major financial markets across the world. Throughout the collection, poems are bathed in the fallout of nuclear and economic terminology.

The title of the book is rich in ambiguous connotations: the bands around the throat seem to focus the debate around lyric stance and the position of the poet. These bands are both constrictions and adornments. Neck and necklaces are dominant images throughout the text: "At the neckline the word you give then / is padlocked by voice print" (*Poems*, p.350) reveals 'Punishment Routines' carefully conflating notions of lyric utterance and constriction. At the time of the writing of this book, the news and newspapers were full of accounts of "necklace murders" in South African townships where a tyre soaked or filled with petrol was placed around the victim's neck and shoulders, and set alight. This form of lynching was a method used by Blacks to execute informers. (see *The Times*, 22 April, 1986, 7/7 and *The Daily Telegraph* 28 May, 1987 10/4 as quoted in O.E.D.). The opening title 'Fool's Bracelet' continues the associations: bracelet was used—in the Seventeenth and Eighteenth centuries—as a slang term for handcuffs, but the dominant imagery of this poem seems to suggest that a fool's bracelet may well be a hangman's noose:

> . . . The star of swords is put upon
> his neck. He falls to the ground. Why not?
> It is a root and branch arrangement, giving
> the keys openly to a provident reversal,
> to net uptake. To these whom we resist.
> To blot out a shabby record by a daze
> intrinsic in transit: *see what is won,*
> *we have cut him down, like the evening sun*
> *His only crown.* Don't you think that's enough
> to peel a larynx at a flotation, they say,
> by the stub of a tuning fork delivery. The issue
> hits all-time peaks in no time at all,
> buy on the rumour, sell on the fact. Only
> a part gives access to the rest, you get
> in at the floor too: *And his dance is gone.*
>
> (*Poems*, p.342).

The "star of swords" suggests an initiatory ritual where each must place their heads within a star formed by the crisscrossing of swordblades so as to risk decapitation. The "root and branch arrangement" punningly suggests both imminent dismemberment or the act of being hung from a tree; certainly the imagery of "uptake", being "cut down" and "his dance" being "gone" suggest the act of being hung and then cut down. The broken neck imaged as "the stub of a tuning fork delivery", and a peeled larynx, are further indications of the book's concern with lyric uterrance and the role of the poet—images significantly interrupted by a voice that registers moral outrage and calls for restraint: "Don't you think that's enough ...They say ...". It is also possible that this last phrase acts as a warning against the lyric voice's propensity to stage its own vulnerability for rhetorical purposes, as it is followed by lines that seem to ironise the urgent loftiness of poetic "issue": "The issue / hits all-time peaks in no time at all, / buy on the rumour and sell on the fact". The "all-time peaks" attained in "no time at all" ironise the cult of the transcendental moment that was so much a hallmark of the "egotistical sublime" of Romantic notions of poetic genius.

The language register of price fluctuation in stocks and shares further undermines the lyric voice's staged vulnerability as a costly rhetorical stance. Prynne is very aware of the problematic claims made on behalf of, and in some instances actually by, (Romantic) poets. His essay 'English Poetry and Emphatical Language' reinforces the critique of Romantic Subjectivity by quoting Lukács' condemnation from his early work *The Theory of the Novel*:

> In lyric poetry, only the great moment exists, the moment at which the meaningful unity of nature and soul or their meaningful divorce, the necessary and affirmed loneliness of the soul becomes eternal. At the lyrical moment the purest interiority of the soul, set apart from duration without choice, lifted above the obscurely-determined multiplicity of things, solidifies into substance; whilst alien, unknowable nature is driven from within, to agglomerate into a symbol that is illuminated throughout. Yet this relationship between soul and nature can be produced only at lyrical moments ... Only in lyric poetry do these direct, sudden flashes of the substance become like lost original manuscripts suddenly made legible; only in lyric poetry is the subject, the vehicle of such experiences, transformed into the sole carrier of meaning, the only true reality
>
> ('English Poetry', p.139).

In *Bands Around The Throat*, Lukács's image of the flashing lyric moment transformed by the poet into a suddenly legible lost manuscript, is bitterly undercut by the imagery of stocks and shares: paper bonds to be cashed in at their peak moment of value—to adopt an idiom entirely appropriate for this dark and violent book: making a killing: "buy on the rumour, sell on the fact". But it is the seemingly innocuous phrase "in no time at all" that unites the various concerns of this poem, and the collection in general. It is not just an allusion to the moment-out-of-time of lyric transcendentalism, ". . . the claimed nobility and anguish of such moments, the trailing remnants of a discredited sacral destiny . . ." to quote the essay 'English Poetry and Emphatical Language' (p.150). As is often the case with Prynne's work, a punning relationship to idiomatic speech seems apparent, and "in no time at all" recalls another phrase that seems right at the heart of this book's concerns: "In the nick of time". This buried phrase unites this book's exploration of the expression and exploitation of privileged rhetoric— and the rhetoric of privilege—that lies at the foundation of the lyric stance, and the accompanying imagery of hanging and punishment. The phrase "in the nick of time" is likely derived from the practice of "neckeverse". Rod Mengham reveals that, in medieval Europe, clergymen arraigned for felony were entitled to claim Benefit of Clergy and therefore become exempt from trial by secular court (*Language*, p. 36). Neckeverse refers to the practice of showing verse in Latin—usually the beginning to psalm 51—to a defendant, whose ability to read it would save him from hanging in the "necke" of time. Later, this privilege of exemption from the sentence might be extended to any who, on their first conviction, could read. This allusion to the power of literacy feeds back into the major preoccupation of this book: how the lyric stance itself relates to a "privilege of exemption": how it deceptively blurs what Prynne has elsewhere referred to as ". . . the difference between the right and the righteous, the pain of loss and the power of pain" ('A Letter To Andrew Duncan', p.105). Few writers have explored the rhetoric of lyric with such ferocity; its self-appointed desire to "speak for" or "on behalf of", and its complicity in the very machinations of power and exploitation that it would speak out against. The sense of wounded utterance that runs through Prynne's work is never allowed to convincingly occupy a pure register of moral outrage. Instead, the focus is self-consciously upon the rhetorical mileage that such a register seeks to exploit. The 'Letter To Andrew Duncan', in retrospect, betrays Prynne's own concern to keep in check the rhetoric of lyric. The following excerpt, with its focus on readerly confusion over voice and address, seems appropriate to the dangers that are deliberately highlighted in *Bands Around The Throat*:

> But nonetheless the reader has to maintain a particular alertness to make out, within the ironical and self-parodic interplay of tones, the difference between the right and the righteous, the pain of loss and the power of pain. Your solicitation of an anticipatory and retrospective fear is so constant that the reader can hardly discover within the sensorium where actual pain begins and does or does not end. That is the classical difficulty for a rhetoricalised instrument: its readiness to claim the privilege of an autonomous occasion which covertly it exploits. How can you give, unless you are to present merely symptomatic malnutrition, what you claim to have taken away—the wheat from beneath the iron.
>
> ('Letter', p.105)

Bands as a collection seems to be concerned with just this difficulty of a rhetoricalised instrument, and seems to demand of the reader this same alertness over how to negotiate the intensity of images of pain and punishment as they bleed into an interplay of ironical and self-parodic tones. The very titles of the poems continually reinforce this play off / pay off stalemate stance: 'No Song No Supper', 'Rates of Return', 'Punishment routines', 'Swallow your Pride'. It is a dead-end that Prynne is all too well aware of:

> The use is: being used, not ethos but pathos; the counter-move is to claim knowledge while leaving unchanged what is known: returning were as tedious, in the familiar diagnosis, as go o'er. And this despite the remorse of political acknowledgement, since the wound gives power in the very moment that it marksout the victim's observed inability to

use it. The anxiety over the use of this power is not false, but is thus disconnected from active ethical consequence: it floods into its objects and into the subject alike. The method is traditionally dead-end, to have in effect no method but only repetition and abruptness. Finally, then, a despairing amor fati presides, its hatefulness the only hope of and for the real
("A Letter To Andrew Duncan", p.106)

The opening poem in *Bands* acts out this dead-end where ". . . the wound gives power in the very moment that it marks out the victim's observed inability to use it". The imagery of the victim in 'Fool's Bracelet' has already been noted, but in lines 7–15 the despairing sense of hate as the only permitted hope is also there—alongside striking imagery concerning the complicity between the pain of loss and the power of pain:

> . . . What
> don't you want, is there no true end
> to grief at joy, casting away deterrent hope
> in a spate of root filling? The upside of the song
> from the valley below excites lock-tremors
> as the crest gets the voice right by proxy,
> non-stick like a teflon throat. To press on
> without fear of explanation, refusing the jab:
> (*Poems*, p.342).

". . . What / don't you want, is there no true end / to grief at joy" scathingly renders a consumer age where desire endlessly proliferates; is manufactured even as the dreams that money can buy. "non-stick like a teflon throat" is a vivid simile for the lyric voice's culpability— its deceptive presentation of itself as immune to the very forces it is simultaneously claiming to be all engulfing. Notions of the poet —even, and especially the "avant-garde" poet—selling just such "product" to an audience that will then glow with the fake sense of indulging desires beyond the jurisdiction of the vulgar market place, has long dogged Prynne's work: and the issue will be returned to later. Birgitta Johansson points to U.S. Congresswoman Patricia Schroeder's description of Ronald Reagan as being a possible source here. He was described as "just like a Teflon frying pan: Nothing sticks to him" (Quoted by Johanssen, p. 180 n. 35). The lyric voice of protest and outrage is particularly dubious for its alignment with two conflicting positions: that of master—of the privileged and specialised instrument of song—and slave: an emotional and political identification with the dispossessed and victimised. This leads to a collusive position where "…Your means are power, that is, but your ends are its overthrow " ("A Letter To Andrew Duncan", p.102). The implication here is that the lyric voice has so much rhetorically invested in the self-righteous alignment with the victimised, that it is wedded to the forces it would overthrow—a poignantly marital phrase that may also chime with the "bands" of the collection's title. The book as a whole constantly conflates the notion of rhetorical investment in certain positions with the economic vocabulary of investment in stocks and shares: hence the "upside of the song" in the lines above, with their ironic allusion to the upward movement of share prices. In fact the poem as a whole filters the rhetoric of lyric transcendentalism through the stock market language of futures and options. The "bands" of the the book's title are also zero-coupon bonds: "Corporate bonds that do not pay interest periodically (semiannually) in the fashion of conventional types of bonds, but instead sell at discounts of par until their final maturity, when payment of principal at par plus all of the interest accumulated (compounded) at the rate specified at the time of original issuance of the bonds is paid in a lump sum" (Charles J. Woelfel. *The Fitzroy Dearborn Encyclopoedia of Banking and Finance*, p.1218). The fact that with such bonds no cash is actually paid out until final maturity is an ironic comment upon the non-stick teflon throat of the lyric which never accounts for its complicities, never counts the cost of its rhetorical privilege. The ever escalating cost, the "upside of the song" that "excites lock-tremors / as the crest gets the voice right by proxy" continues this idea: the "lock-tremors" are both an image of a barely containable flood of lyric intensity, and an acknowledgement that the attraction of zero-coupon bonds for investors is "…the locking in of the prevailing high interest at issuance of the bonds" (Woelfel, p.1218). Getting the voice right by proxy, seems again to chide at the privileged rhetorical instrument of lyric and its self-elected authorisation to speak for another. The idea that there is disingenuous pretence at the heart of lyric aspiration has long haunted Prynne's work. As his 'Reader's Lockjaw' article suggests: "The disguise is to want not to lose; the reality is not to get left holding a want you cannot steer (hypocritical detachment, say)" (p.73). Elements of this disguise emerge in lines already quoted: "What / don't you want, is there no true end / to grief at joy, casting away deterrent hope / in a spate of root filling", These lines contain a similar ambivalence to those that close the book that preceded *Bands*; *The Oval Window*.

> . . . The years
> jostle and burn up as a trust plasma.
> Beyond help it is joy at death itself:
> a toy hard to bear, laughing all night.
>   (*Poems*, p.339)

Here there is a sense of joy at defeat, and a certain vertigo of being "Beyond help" resulting in the possible hysteria of "laughing all night". In *The Oval Window*, images of shifting balance recur as part of that poem's concern with the information processing activities of the inner ear and the shifting of otolith crystals to orient the human organism. The lines from *Bands* introduce a significantly nuclear dimension to the problem, with the phrase "deterrent hope". Prynne's sense of poetic stalemate in this—perhaps his bitterest—collection, is framed by the precarious balance of world power maintained by the Cold War. Blake, in 'The Human Abstract'—a poem written in the 1790's when the omniscient eye of the English state needed to suppress dissident forces supporting the French Revolution—well understood that fear was the vital ingredient in preserving social "order". Blake's line "And mutual fear brings peace" prophetically describes the Cold War dynamic, and Prynne's phrase "deterrent hope" adds a further twist. Throughout the collection images of hope and hopelessness are played off against each other. Hope is given a mock religious dimension, being constantly juxtaposed against, and often fused with, the language of stock market economics: particularly the language of futures and options. This process begins in the opening lines of 'Fool's Bracelet':

In the day park shared by advancement
the waiting clients make room, for another
rising bunch of lifetime disposals. It is
the next round in the sing-song by treble touches
a high start not detained by the option
of a dream to pass right on through . . .

(Poems, p.342)

These opening lines suggest to me an ironised contemplation of death and the attendant hope for an afterlife: "a dream to pass on through". Reeve and Kerridge have also drawn attention to the opening line of 'Rates of Return'—"Here then admit one at a time"—as suggesting "both the gates of heaven and admission to some cultural spectacle" (*Nearly Too Much*, p.34). Similarly, the opening lines from "Fool's Bracelet" give us the contemporary scene as a society of the spectacle imaged as "the day park", and the souls awaiting possible afterlife are deemed "waiting clients"; satirically extending the 80s' conversion of all aspects of life into "service industries", to religion. The irony operating throughout this collection is that both Christianity and investment banking have a vested interest in the "futures market". Hence the merged vocabularies of hope and expectation: for an afterlife, and rising share prices. Both involve a postponement in the evaluation of the present in favour of future rewards, and so the present—"the day park"—is "shared by advancement". If "advancement" might signal ironical commentary on the state of civilisation and its discontents as an inventory of financial gain, the fact that it is "shared" brings further poignancy. The term "shared" blurs a vocabulary of reciprocal relationships and communal commitment with the opposite vocabulary of the division of a company's capital entitling the limited few to a proportion of the profits. The blurred registers of hope and expectation continue as: "It is / the next round in the sing-song by treble touches, / a high start not detained by the option / of a dream to pass right on through". Christian notions that the fulfilment of the dream of an afterlife—the "next round"—is the preserve of an elect is also mirrored in the organizations of "futures exchanges". *The Fitzroy Dearborn Encyclopedia of Banking and Finance* explains that:

Generally, membership in an exchange is individual, and only
members can buy and sell futures contracts on the trading
floor where a "pit" or "ring" is designated for the trading of
each commodity. Bids and offers are made by open outcry.
Members are permitted to trade for their own account as
position traders or day traders

(p.505)

The commodification of hope as a religious contract for the future—
an afterlife bought into through a slow-maturing policy demanding
unquestioning suffering in this world—relates back to the phrase
"deterrent hope". Hope for an afterlife—conditional upon the results
of the day of judgement, and therefore a certain quota of fear—acts
like a nuclear deterrent in its cementing of the social order by implicit
threat: that of Nuclear apocalypse or damnation. Prynne's introduction
of this parallel is characteristically ambiguous and ambivalent in tone:
providing the reader with exactly the difficulties in discerning "the
difference between the right and the righteous, the pain of loss and
the power of pain" amongst the ironical and parodic interplay of tones
that he felt problematic in his letter to Andrew Duncan:

> ... What
> don't you want, is there no true end
> to grief at joy, casting away deterrent hope
> in a spate of root filling?
> (*Poems*, p.342)

Is the "casting away" here part of the recognition that the attraction of
hope relies precisely upon it remaining unrealised; upon it remaining
an endlessly deferred desire? In a letter to Drew Milne, to be returned
to later, Prynne claims that "The danger point about paradise was not
that it wasn't attractive ... but that it wasn't satisfactory: a defect shielded
from the tests of *sic et non* because of the indefinite postponement
attached to the definition" (*Parataxis*, p.58). And yet the "casting away"
here is contextualized by being "in a spate of root filling": here the
cementing of social order through fear is cruelly figured through the
imagery of dental surgery and fillings; most people's most potent image

of pain. Of course, such an image of the mouth relates to Prynne's wider preoccupation with wounded utterance.

The kind of vocabulary evident in the quotation given from *The Fitzroy Dearborn Encyclopaedia* is used to open the second poem in the series, "No Song No Supper":

> Even so by open outcry across
> this ring a deep frost cuts up
> a halo of grey cinders; the night
> is stark cold to pay less and less
> (*Poems*, p.343)

Here we have the bidding and offering conducted by the floor brokers of the trading "ring" offset by imagery suggestive of the nuclear disaster at Chernobyl: "a halo of grey cinders" connotes the spread of radiation fallout, and in fact "gray" (spelt with an "a" and abbreviated to GY) is "a unit of radiation dose, equivalent to the absorption of one Joule of energy into one kilogram of matter, and equal to 100 rads" (*Something in the Wind*, p.236). The status of the myriad specialist discourses threaded through Prynne's work has always been a central bone of contention. Bakhtinian heteroglossia? Postmodern collapse of grand narratives? "Legitimation crisis"? An elegiac modernist "shoring" of fragments against contemporary ruin? All these positions have tempted various critics, and all in some way return to the issue— pun intended—and status of voice in this poetry. Interestingly, Peter Gould's *Fire in the Rain: The Democratic Consequences of Chernobyl* uses the nuclear accident in Russia to highlight what he calls the "process of intellectual fission" (p.ix) that characterises our age, but which he claims has been escalating since the dissolution of Natural philosophy in the seventeenth century. Gould claims that offsetting general trends towards increased specialisation and fragmentation are the sciences of "human space and time": geography and history. These disciplines, considered through Gould's desired holism, are like "shepherds of the intellectual world" rounding up the strays of fractured knowledge. Gould's choice of imagery is, intentionally or otherwise, suggestively Christian with its shepherd / flock analogy. Reeve and Kerridge pay attention to "Rates of Return" as throwing "Christian allegory into crisis" (*Nearly Too Much*, p.143) with its imagery of "the sights of growth from immortal seed / acting like fallout on upland pastures / causing restrictions on the movement of sheep" (*Poems* p.345).

The usefulness of Gould's analysis of the Chernobyl accident for a reading of Prynne, lies in its focus upon the feedback between human and environmental relationships: 'An event of the physical world, caused by the human, and rebounding back on the living world, lay squarely in that human-environment cleft where things have to be brought together in order to understand what is really going on.' (*Fire in the Rain* p.X). It is when Gould uses radiation as his metaphor for examining the far reaching effects of this Nuclear disaster, that the connections with Prynne are most productive:

> Today, in modern medicine, radio-isotopes are used in minute quantities as tracers to disclose invisible structures within the human body—brain tumors, clogged arteries, connections and obstructions of all sorts. In some strange but similar way, the radioactive fallout from Chernobyl has also served as a tracer, moving through the physical and living worlds to disclose their chains of connection. It has also crossed over those connections to reveal some startling thing about the structures of the bodies politic in all their bureaucratic power. In neither case—real fallout moving through living structures or figurative fallout moving on political structures—are the effects healthy or reassuring. Both living bodies and bodies politic are capable of developing malignancies. The fallout of Chernobyl disclosed not only grave problems for human health, but equally grave problems for democracies relying increasingly upon bureaucratized government informed by industrial and scientific power. In neither case is the story a pretty or commendable one as we trace it across the structures connecting the physical, living, and all-too-human worlds together. To the degree that we can keep these intact in our thinking, and refuse to defuse the issues by disconnecting and partitioning them in traditional ways, so a larger understanding can inform and strengthen democratic society itself.
>
> (*Fire in the Rain*, pp.x–xi)

Bands' wilfully impure discourse, bathed in the fallout of nuclear and economic terminology, is a poetic tracer disclosing the complicities of lyric outrage. Where Gould writes of the 'human-environment cleft where things have to be brought together in order to understand 'what is really going on', Prynne's haunted sense that we have induced moral mutation of the species has resulted in poetic utterance's cleft palate. The connections between bodies living and politic has been a major concern of Prynne's work since its early focus upon "liminal" travellers such as Aristeas in 'Aristeas, In Seven Years', to the focus upon the individual body's capacity for regenerative response and the body politic's need to generate responsibility in *Wound Response*. In the already-quoted 'The Ideal Star-Fighter', the "moral mutation" diagnosed is aligned with a skewing of the relationship between these two bodies:

> Now a slight meniscus floats on the moral
>   pigment of these times, producing
> displacement of the body image, the politic
>   albino.
>   (*Poems*, p.165)

In the opening of 'Marzipan', from *Bands*, this blanching of the body politic has become a desolate image of spectral existence worryingly akin to Dante and Eliot:

> We poor shadows light up again
> slowly now in the wasted province
> where colours fall and are debated
> through a zero coupon, the de-
> funct tokens in a soft regard.
>   (*Poems*, p.347)

The skewed relationship between individual body and body politic in this "wasted province" seems to have as its only bond the dubious mediating force of the "zero coupon". Given the somewhat purgatorial connotations of "we poor shadows" as potential shades, the zero coupon as a bond in which the investor receives only one payment at maturity seems again to continue the uneasy parallel between Christian religion's and a market economy's mutual interest in "futures and options". The title 'Marzipan' remains obscure. The poem's individual appearance as part of Peter Riley's *Poetical Histories* series, may provide a clue. In this publication, Prynne's poem was accompanied by a translation of the poem into French by the poet Bernard Dubourg titled "massepain". It seems likely that Prynne's title itself becomes a pun on its French equivalent as "mass pain". Its status as luxury foodstuff—literally the icing on the cake—returns to the ambiguous status of the "bands" of the whole collection's title as being both constrictions and adornment. "Marzipan" as a title is part of the book's scrutiny of the lyric rhetoric of pained outcry as being dubiously confectionary: and of the capacity of such rhetoric to complicitly sweeten the pill that it claims to be spitting out. Hence the irony in the title of the final poem in the collection: "Swallow your Pride" (*Poems*, p.347).

"Marzipan" as a title may also ironically allude to the pasting of natural resources as a result of the reactor explosion at Chernobyl. Certainly the fifth stanza presents apocalyptic images suggestive of the fire in the reactor that burned for five days, consuming at least 10 percent of the reactor core (*Something in the Wind*, p.4):

> Now red dust hangs, and fire drives
> the gold star into a dark vapour.
> To mark out the pitch of ennui
> a strong sense of, well, woodsmoke
> in due season makes its offering:

The image of the gold star obscured by dark vapour is suggestive: a gold star has connotations of an award—and possibly ironically alludes to the insistence upon the safety of nuclear energy that the industry constantly reinforces. "Ennui" has obviously literary connotations of a rather mannered *fin de siècle* spiritual boredom—but here this emotion is anchored to "woodsmoke". It reminds us that the "wasted province" is not just a modern consumer-hell, but is also the forested wetlands on the border between the Ukraine and Byelorussia: land famed for its natural beauty. The "ennui" may well be that displayed by the Soviet

Union towards the occupants of such territory. Evacuations of some of the most dangerous zones, such as the district of Narodichi, had not taken place as late as a month after the catastrophe. Other villages were placed under strict control, told only to eat "clean food" that never reached them. Milk, vegetables and meat from certain regions was admitted to be contaminated, and sent elsewhere to be "treated". Of course, no one informed the village inhabitants that such precautions were futile in view of the fact that the wood being burnt for fuel and heating was as contaminated as the foodstocks. This may account for the lines "a strong sense of, well, woodsmoke / in due season makes its offering:" : especially as the accident at Chernobyl occurred at the approach of the May Day Festival in the towns and villages of Ukraine, Byelorussia, Russia and the Baltic lands. As Russian journalist Alla Yaroshinskaya retrospectively described the scene:

> ... all over the country, as in previous years, millions of people lined the streets. It was extremely hot. Not just mild, but hot. Children dressed in national costume, breathing radioactive fumes, danced on the Kreschatik, the main street of the Ukranian capital. On the stand, greeting the crowds, stood members of the Ukranian Politburo, government ministers, and invited guests. At almost precisely the same moment, senior civil servants were hurrying their children to Borispol airport to get them away from the scene of the catastrophe. The children of the betrayed workers and intellectuals were left behind to delight the eyes of the ministers; this was the price paid to give international opinion the illusion that all is well.
>
> (*Chernobyl: The Forbidden Truth*, p.17)

The final five stanzas of 'Marzipan' have much in common with Prynne's elegy for Paul Celan 'Es Lebe Der König' from *Brass*. This stately but foreboding poem opens with a semi-mythical, apocalyptic landscape where "Fire and honey oozes from cracks in the earth", and contains lines that are already ambivalently marking the pitch of ennui: "Give us this love of murder and / sacred boredom, you walk in the shade of the technical house" (*Poems*, p.170). The final half of

'Marzipan' recalls this savaging of the Lord's prayer, and presents a
materialised version of 'Es Lebe der König''s landscape, giving us a
picture of humanity as shades walking in the debris of the technical
house of advancement:

> ... *Vorsprung durch EDV*,
> as mother knows, there is no rose,
> as in abandoned markets and deserted streets
> wheat sprouts flourish. The pretext
>
> of small mercies, seasonal rebate in
> the loose change: as though they were
> sieving the very soil itself! Attuned
> to modest airs the conductor beats
> time to flattened repeats. All over
>
> The same again not held back, to ask grace
> at a graceless face it is our own
> in the glass of dark recall, seen
> at love all in the replay; the heartland
> is dug out for a life underneath
>
> In broadest, magical daylight. You see
> as in late spring, shrouding in mist,
> the bright, smooth water. The price
> is right, *eau minérale naturelle*
> from the hypermarket and thousands
>
> of feet of glacial sand. Then thousand
> families in the mountains, starved
> on mountain grass: and made me eat
> both gravel, dirt and mud, and last
> of all, to gnaw my flesh and blood.
>
> (*Poems*, p.348)

The enigmatic "technical house" of 'Es Lebe der König' has become
the irony of *Vorsprung durch EDV*. Contemporaneously with Prynne's

collection, Audi were advertising their cars with the slogan "Progress through Technology"—making a ghastly connection between the gas chambers of the Celan elegy and the Chernobyl fallout as ciphers of technological progress. The meaning of the acronym EDV is suitably overdetermined. It might be the German acronym for Electronic Data Processing (*elektronische Datenverarbeitung*), as *The Oval Window* explicitly uses materials from information processing. It might stand for Emission Data Vehicle: the testing of exhaust emissions being rendered suitably absurd in the light of the emissions emanating from Chernobyl. These emissions are themselves filtered through the contaminated vocabularies of religion and economics: "The Pretext / of small mercies, seasonal rebate in / the loose change: as though they were / sieving the soil itself !" Radiation is certainly loose change, and indeed the reaction to the threat of contamination was exactly to sieve the soil, as stanza 11 has it "the heartland / is dug out for a life underneath". As Louis Mackay and Mark Thompson explain:

> During the first ten days after the accident, 72 villages near Chernobyl were evacuated and abandoned for good. The decontamination measures carried out during the summer and autumn included the removal of topsoil from the most seriously affected areas, both inside and outside the exclusion zone; what was done with the topsoil is not known.
>
> (*Something in the Wind*, p.5)

The musical image of the "conductor" beating time to "flattened repeats" darkly disguises the blipping of Geiger counters, and such "repeats" mark the overloaded monotony of "All over /the same again not held back"—only to then become the "replay" possibly of television sets imaged as "the glass of dark recall"; what Jameson has called the "moebius strip of the media". Even the potential pastoral image of seeing ". . . as in late spring, shrouded in mist, / the bright smooth water" is tainted. Peter Gould points out that Sweden was the first to detect Chernobyl and warn Europe; and its and Norway's hydroelectric programs have produced picturesque lakes in glaciated valleys that are potential "cesium sinks" for retaining nuclear fallout in the form of sediment at lake bottoms. The "thousands of feet of glacial sand" refers to the 5,000 tons of sand, clay, lead and dolomite that were dropped from the air onto the Chernobyl reactor in the first five days of the fire (*Something in the Wind*, p.4). The poem ends by indicating the human cost of the tragedy; and most strikingly introduces a "me" of indefinable status whose only response is horrific auto-cannibalism: "... and made me eat both gravel, dirt and mud, and last / of all, to gnaw my flesh and blood".

What marks out Prynne's work as separate from many other "avant-garde" writers is the degree of scepticism he has towards not just the rhetorical stance of the lyric, but equally the stance of the avant-garde as being similarly predicated upon a heroic rhetoric of risk. Such an idealised rhetoric of risk-taking sits uneasily alongside the relatively comfortable conditions of artistic production in the liberal west, and problematises the nature of the "freedom" it pertains to be fighting for. Prynne accepts the aptness of the model of market economics for discussing contemporary avant-garde poetics, but not from a perspective of "resistance" to that model. Much has been made of "Language" writing's endeavour to re-define reader-writer relations, and in the process to convert passive consumption to active production. However, for Prynne, this claim seems problematised for two reasons: firstly for its assumption that there can be a safe-haven from which to resist such forces, and secondly: that resistance itself can be an attack. Prynne favours the model of market economics precisely because its scope encompasses the commodification of both freedom and dissent. The 'Letter to Ashley Hayles' asks:

> ... consumption to be renamed as production: the open text, the inventive, selective reader, free to opt for useful waste or wasteful utility ... Isn't it the classic freedom to eat cake, to diversify an assumed leisure and to choose out of a diversity which is precisely the commodity-spectacle of a pre-disposed array, clearwrapped in unitised portion control?

This essay has explored Prynne's unease at the rhetoric of privilege upholding the lyric stance. And yet, he seems to find a not dissimilar rhetoric submerged within the "language" project: a notion of the specialised, elect readership who will receive their just rewards. In this way—perhaps curiously alongside a nostalgic vision of a pre-capitalist world where labour and reward are re-connected—"language" writing is seen "to provide a rewarding increase in benefits for those defined as deserving (earning) (acquiring) them" ('Letter to Ashley Hayles'). For Prynne, the appropriateness of the model of market economics is not that it redefines writer-reader relations as a pact of resistance to those forces, but that it re-inscribes these relations as being complicit within such forces. In the 'Letter to Allen Fisher' he discusses *Down Where Changed* in revealing terms:

> At the historical moment of that book I believed it necessary to poke about in the reader's appetite for guilty remorse just as much as for salved conscience, given that each so easily converts into the other (by a sort of vicious, mechanical glee). The author's sternness is of course also a surrender, to hard-line market forces in the retailing of the unwanted. All the appetites feed off the same ersatz nourishment; the underlying confidence that there are securely enough alternative menus to provide inexhaustible choice. That, too, is the consumer's name for dialectic: the advertiser's apocalypse, downhill all the way.
>
> (*Parataxis* 8/9, pp.157–158)

Earlier in the same letter he explains that "The reader's freedom was to be constantly interfered with, as an invidious commodity; pretending that there had been no immunity to the violence and yet also noticing that pretence as just that" (p.157). This seems also true of *Bands Around the Throat*—except that here the stakes are upped: not only is the reader's freedom interfered with, but so is the writer's, and most particularly any sense that the writer is immune and detached from what is described. The bands around the throat squeeze the rhetoric of lyric privilege until it wheezes its complicity in a ghastly death-rattle. The poem 'Punishment Routines' converts the capital punishment imagery of 'Fool's Bracelet' into the punishment of capital, substituting poetic immunity for impurity:

> At the neckline the word you give then
> is padlocked by voiceprint, by neat cement
> on the impurity radius sweeping the lexicon
> as if to say eagerly, go on go on . . .
>
> (*Poems*, p.350)

This eager anticipation almost mocks readerly expectation as it is simultaneously manipulating it: we are hanging on the poem's every word, but so is Prynne. This collection is exactly about the need to situate the poet within the frame, and to disallow the disguise of hypocritical detachment. It is concerned with pealing the teflon coating off the larynx and making things stick. Its precariousness—and perhaps this is the central question not here discussed—centres on the status and function of irony in Prynne's work. It is a precarious balance that remains unresolved in his work, and is particularly dramatised in *Bands*. The 'Letters to Drew Milne' are still preoccupied by a sense of stalemate: "Shoot into the foot, I say, and only then into the air" a statement quickly qualified by: "But the honour of exhausted defeat is such a come-on!" (p.62). As the closing line of 'Punishment Routines' has it: "Eat little / and speak less, bleeding inside the mouth" (*Poems*, p.350).

BIBLIOGRAPHY

Gould, Peter. *Fire in the Rain: The Democratic Consequences of Chernobyl.* Cambridge: Polity, 1990.

Johansson, Birgitta. *The Engineering of Being: an Ontological Approach to J.H. Prynne.* Umeå Studies in the Humanities, Umeå, Sweden: Distributed by Swedish Science Press, Uppsala, 1997.

Mackay, Louis, and Thompson, Mark eds. *Something in the Wind: Politics After Chernobyl.* London: Pluto, for European Nuclear Disarmament [END] in collaboration with the Transnational Insitute [TNI], 1998.

Mengham, Rod *Language.* London, Fontana Press, 1993.

Prynne, J.H. 'A Letter to Andrew Duncan.' *Grosseteste Review15, 1983–84*

Prynne, J.H. 'A Letter to Steve McCaffery.' *The Gig 7, November 2000.*

Prynne, J.H. 'A Letter to Allen Fisher.' *Parataxis 8/9, 1996.*

Prynne, J.H. 'English Poetry and Emphatical Language.' *Proceedings of the British Academy,* Vol. LXXIV; 1988 (Oxford University Press, 1989).

Prynne, J.H. *Poems.* Tarset: Bloodaxe Books, 2005.

Prynne, J.H. 'Reader's Lockjaw.' *Perfect Bound* 5, 1978.

Prynne, J.H. / Drew Milne, 'Some Letters.' *Parataxis* 5, Winter 1993–4.

Reeve, Neil and Kerridge, Richard. *Nearly Too Much: The Poetry of J.H. Prynne.* Liverpool: Liverpool University Press, 1995.

Woelfel, Charles J. *The Fitzroy Dearborn Encyclopedia of Banking and Finance.* 10th ed. Chicago: Fitzroy Dearborn, 1994.

Yaroshinskaya, Alla. *Chernobyl: The Forbidden Truth.* trans Michèle Kahn, Julia Sallabank; Photographs by M. Metzel. Oxford: Jon Carpenter, 1994.

XL Prynne

Keston Sutherland

> . . . the ques-
> tion is really what *size* we're in, how much of
> it is the measure, at one time.[1]

> On the march. Simmer down . . .[2]

What is radical thinking? Is there radical thinking in J.H. Prynne's poems? What is anyone looking *for*?

There is no one person to ask. There is not even one Marx. "Man," wrote one of them (the twenty-five year old Marx of 1843–4) "is *the world of man.*" Then, several steps later in the adventure of his manuscript, this same Marx tried out a still more poetical and now famous phrase: "To be radical is to grasp things by the root. But for man the root is man himself."[3] Radikal sein, *to be radical*—is to grasp. What kind of act is this *grasp*, this *fassen* urged in the infinitive that resembles a state of being? It is understanding transformed by recognition, recognition transformed by understanding. The radical grasp, for Marx, is not the mere *use* of a recognition and an understanding that are fixed "faculties" imperturbable by their objects. To be radical, the grasp must be the act in which each transforms both. This reciprocal transformation of recognition and understanding is one thing that distinguishes radical thinking from its real and imagined alternatives.[4] Radical thinking, for *this* Marx, is thus an activity different from religious or conservative thinking not merely in temperament but in kind. It must itself produce the person capable of it. It does this through its passion and through its relationship with its object. Radical thinking must understand the world by understanding the root of it, and it must recognise that this root is man; recognition and understanding here transform and illuminate each other; but what is it that they grasp in this transforming act? The root, says Marx, which is man himself. Man as the root is however a difficult object to grasp. Far from being "outside the world" or even distinguishable from it, man *is* the world, or at least, he is the world that belongs to and is intelligible to him, what Marx called *das Diesseits*: "this" world.[5] He is not a root that thinking can clip off.[6] Is all the world, then, its own root? The world must be grasped by the root, but this root by which the world must be grasped is man, and man is the world.

Is radical thinking then deliverance into one of those hermeneutic circles that Heidegger believed thinking must be intrepid enough to remain inside? Is it a "closed circle" that we must "get to grips with," as Prynne's words order us to and threaten that we will, pathogenically echoing Heidegger?[7]

Man is the root | man is the world. If we want to read these two moments of poetic arguing by Marx as coordinated insights into "the truth of this world," "die *Wahrheit des Diesseits*," as he earlier distinguishes the truth that interests him, rather than to read them as two differential, passionate expressions of the same creative impulse "to unmask . . . the *holy form* of self-estrangement" practiced under the name of religion;[8] if, that is, we want to read Marx fairly strictly as an author of philosophical *propositions*, in whose work the ambivalence of propositions is to be understood as a failure of cognitive consistency rather than as art; if we want to read Marx that way, then what he is saying here is that *das Diesseits* is *die Wurzel*: the root is this whole. In our best possible grasp of it, all the world we truly need is radical.[9] Is radical thinking then capable of grasping—and must it by extension always implicitly grasp—any and every object, no matter what its function or substance, no matter what its size?

Marx, like many other thinkers, names as "radical" an act of thinking that, besides being the kind of transforming reciprocation between "faculties" already described, at once both increases and diminishes its proper object of inquiry. Radical thinking has at once both a greater and a smaller object than religious thinking. Both sorts of thinking count as their object both man and the world. But the object of radical thinking is greater, because man is no longer merely the narrow creature who suffers in a pinching and oppressive universe, inquiring if he dare disturb it, or, more smartly, ventriloquising that question and laughing at it in *vers libre*; he is the world. His lyricism is not a petition. Man then is a greater object for radical thinking. The object of radical thinking is at the same time smaller, because "this world," the world of man, is established in its truth only "once the *other-world of truth*," that is, the illusory world of religious thinking, "has vanished."[10] In other words, the object of radical thinking is just one world and not two (or more). To call on people "to give up their illusions about their condition," Marx writes, "is to *call on them to*

105

give up a condition that requires illusions."[11] There is no more need of a counter-earth, no inspiration point from which to toss a "backward | glance at the planet."[12] I am greater by the measure of what I lose. For radical thinking, then, man is greater, because he is the world; but for the same thinking, the world is smaller, because it is man; and together in their single identity, world and man are the root that must be grasped, greater and smaller at once.[13]

Marx calls on us to abandon that life which self-estrangement and illusions have reduced to exorbitance. Prynne's poem 'The Numbers,' the first formal lesson of *Kitchen Poems*, makes a parallel demand: "We must shrink." Why must we? "*That*" life, the poem tells us, is too diffuse and must yield to *this*, to Marx's *Diesseits*: "There is no other | *beginning* on power."[14] Not just any thinking will issue this "call," as Marx describes it, or so imperatively determine "the first essential," in Prynne's phrase.[15] It is radical thinking that issues this call. In other words, radical thinking makes our condition, our *Zustand*, life or world, smaller by the discipline of cognitive restriction and the relinquishment of "illusions" about it, leaving us with *this* life alone; and at the same time it aggrandizes that restricted condition by immensely increasing its sufficiency, its independent viability and its adequateness, what in some theoretical lexicons would be called its autonomy, and by making life or the world more truthful, beautiful or liveable.[16] I am smaller by the measure of what I gain.

Neither this nor any Marx will preside over the thoughts that follow in this essay. My subject is radical thinking in Prynne. I begin with these ambivalently propositional, ambivalently poetic moments of arguing[17] from the *Contribution to the Critique of Hegel's Philosophy of Right* not because they are original or particularly influential within the tradition of thinking I will discuss; I begin with them because they are one example, among numberless others ranging at least from Parmenides to Judith Butler, of how "man," or subjectivity, or woman, or the person, is represented or made available as an object for "radical thinking" through either the implicit or the directly presented question of what size he is and what size his world is.[18]

This may seem a position of inordinate or even surplus abstraction from which to begin a discussion of radical thinking. If we are looking for radical thinking in Prynne, should we not start with the realities of injustice and the material distribution of power, and ask what is in fact thought about them by this poetry? Would that not be a study more likely to yield an account of Prynne's "materialism?"[19] Prynne does sometimes have graphic designs on the realities of injustice, staging a confrontation between real suffering and the compound mechanisms of our appetite for it. 'Refuse Collection' is in part a grotesquely frictionless skid through numerous reports of sexual torture and mutilation in Abu Ghraib, its anger as flushed and crude as its knowledge is syndicated; and Prynne's latest book, *To Pollen*, includes in its portfolio of exotic noumena "a father racked | in misery and bearing like a gift his crushed and | bloodied son," the anonymous human footage of any number of massacres in Iraq.[20] If there is radical thinking in Prynne, must not its basis be these points of explicit contact with social injustice? Is there not somewhere in all of Prynne's poetry a realist *text*, however compressed or deviantly rationed, on which the long passages of obscure circumscript are a kind of darkly aberrant or negative *commentary*? It may be tempting to think so.[21] The proof and guarantee of radical thinking could then be *realism*, the disruptive jutting in of illuminated social fact. *Her Weasels Wild Returning*, I could then say, is about the return to action of F-4G SAM hunter jets in the Gulf War of 1990–91: this is the *text*, and whatever the sentence "Dart laps French too" may mean *later*, for *now* at least it can be sorted into the category of *comment*.[22] But Prynne's poetry is not easily rescheduled into realism as radical illumination shadowed by a paradoxical and anti-realist exegesis; and one reason for this is of course that realism is violently and intensely distrusted by this poetry. Flashes of what seems like documentary realism in Prynne's late work are impossible to accept simply as "flashes of where we are," to lift a phrase from 'The Ideal Star-Fighter,' however brute their mimicry or unprettified their transcription. A poem from *Triodes* spells this out, stencilling realism and its alternatives into a moral diagram that reduces them both to parallel channels whose switching device is bathos:

> Meet and make a match on the pedigree as follows.
> Imagine any triode as being replaced
> by an equivalent diode,

>   mapping out the anode potential on tender
>   factored to Mozambique sugar rehab,
>   total funded in package *per pro*:
>   1. The Kuwait Fund for Arab Economic Development;
>   2. The Opec Fund for International Development;
>   3. The Arab Bank for Economic Development in Africa;
>   4. Nedcor Bank Limited;
>   5. Acucareira de Xinavane S.A.R.L.
> The anode potential produces the same effect
>   in the region near the cathode
>   as the combined effects of anode and grid
>   in the corresponding triode.
> Oil to sugar the map beds out, open and shut,
>   doves fall out of the sky.
>
> (Poems, p.498)

In a moral universe that runs on replacement by equivalents, distinction is alternation. Farce is everything and nothing, smaller is the new greater, every line-break is a surplus mandating *vice-versa*: "everything titillates to the contrary."[23] The numbers here stacked up as a list are no longer those of Prynne's much earlier poem, 'L'Extase de M. Poher.'[24] They are not the refractories of a scientific realism rubbishing the lyricism on which they trespass, *Steroid Metaphrast* vs. *Fondling*, since "lyricism" is here already held at implicit bullet point throughout. They are not the moments of truth, they are its banners and competition entry codes. Scratch off "Nedcor Bank Limited," what is underneath? Congratulations, you have won one free recognition. To upgrade from inert to transforming, send off now for the whole brochure.

What then do we do with our "father racked | in misery" if we cannot take his appearance in the poem for the radical illumination of suffering? He is not just a "familiar || whipping toy" that "forms as a habit" in the mind condemned to extort pathos from its own projections; there is real pathos in this figure whom we do know to be real.[25] But what does the pathos mean if the realism that grants it to us is radically indistinguishable from alternative uses of language that point at and describe nothing real? If we read this father and bloodied son as *suffering truly voiced*, we might say that their appearance in the poem fulfills what Adorno called the "condition of all truth."

> Das Bedürfnis, Leiden beredt werden zu lassen, ist Bedingung aller Wahrheit.
>
> *The need to lend a voice to suffering is a condition of all truth.*[26]

Not realism, then, but the release of real suffering into eloquence, in this case by realistic means, would be the radical illumination and the justified promise of its pathos. But the truthfulness of this voice given to suffering is itself the problem in Prynne's poetry from *Brass* downward. The problem is not that the voice given to suffering is in fact untruthful, so that we disbelieve it; that would be a problem simply of weak imitation, of insincerity, of propaganda or of scepticism concerning the truth content of poetic verisimilitude (the scapegoat signifier and its vicissitudes). For Prynne's poetry, the problem is more deeply intractable. It is that "we are immune to disbelief."[27] Once realism is discounted as radical illumination, the voice given to suffering is believed to be truthful both if it is successful on the terms of realism and if it is unsuccessful on those terms; and that is both what makes possible a moral anthropology untied from realism as its foundation and terminal emphasis, *and* what makes pathos so treacherous. The condition of all truth is unavoidably rigged up so as to be met in advance by a proleptic assent posing as "instinct," because our belief in this truth is not a radical act, it is our definition of health. We cannot live without believing that *some* voice we know (and own) has been given to the suffering of others, and that this voice is truthful; and so what Adorno calls a "need" and a "condition" are worn through by us to a bare *necessity*, in the sense that food is a necessity: it is what we always buy. Or it is what someone else always buys for us.

This was not always a problem for Prynne, and his poetry was not from its beginning condemned to be the moral anthropology of the consumerism of suffering. The "arab takeaway larder" of *Pearls That Were* comes *after* the founding of Ierusalem, when, as the vertically dissected epigraph to *The Oval Window* tells us, "AFTER is normalized."[28] In *Kitchen Poems* and *The White Stones* this immunity to disbelief, insofar as it is even partly recognised, is a simple fact about who we are and as such a contribution to the panegyric of being, as 'Against Hurt' unconvincingly makes plain, despite its awkward homage to Olson's syntax of cognitive intersections:

> Endowed with so much
> suffering, they should be / and that
> they are so—the pain in the head
>   which applies to me
>
> (Poems, p.52)

Appliance of pain, acquisition of love. It will go on because it is "in the head," and if we are the head, we are also the crown. The suffering of "the others" is, in the human universe of the mid-1960s, part of our own ontological constitution: "quality *is* their presence," Prynne insists in 'Concerning Quality, Again.' But that poem is the last of Prynne's in which a passage of autobiographical realism is presented as the radical illumination of someone else's suffering, the last to fashion from the poet's own tranquil recollection of his own belief a brotherly antiphon summoning pathos and light (the sky and its "pathic glow," the "bright | thread of colour across the dashboard"—or as 'A Dream of Retained Colour' later puts it, with overdue but also with duly bitter sardony, "Lucifer, with- | out any street lamps or TV.").[29] Prynne's moral anthropology of the consumerism of suffering, initiated in earnest and in violent burlesque with *Brass*, begins flickeringly to be tested out in the second half of *The White Stones*. As early as 'Song in Sight of the World,' Prynne mimics a narrator who diagnoses our cannibalism, and even in this early poem it is because "we shall eat them" that the people of realist narrative, the "grey | people walking towards the restaurant," are not real for any radical grasp;[30] but if the unilluminated grey person is the only one on the menu in *The White Stones*, this is not a problem that leaves us biting the air, since there is another person who is *not* on this or any other menu, who *is* alive and who lives not in the restaurant but in the world, and *this* is who we are.

I diminish the world by disowning the exorbitance of realist illumination. I am greater by the measure of *us* whom I do not eat but am. Is the question of size then a simple question of economy? Can we, as 'A Gold Ring Called Reluctance' counsels, avoid eating each other simply by eating slowly and, with good autonomous manners, refusing the extra helping?[31] We must shrink, demanded 'The Numbers;' "we should | shrink," echoes 'The Ideal Star-Fighter' from across the fracture of *Brass*; but the smaller person, greater by the measure of what he loses, is by this later poem identified as the person who knows that he must shrink not just from the luxuriations of realism but from "lethal cupidity."[32] We cannot grasp man as the root just by *loving* him over and beyond his cameos in realism. Pathos is lethal to the object by the measure of the distance from the object that it both invents and commands, regardless of whether the object is painted in Realistic Grey or Pathic Glow Yellow.[33] If there is radical thinking in Prynne's poetry it will not be explained simply by pointing at illustrations of trauma, nor by deciding that the victims of illustrated trauma are loveable. The poetry itself repeatedly tells us this and it is right. Implicit in each of those illustrations is the prodding catechistical line break that commences the fourth stanzaic procedure of 'Nothing Like Examples:' "why not | believe this?" I choose not to believe it, the poem itself dutifully answers, because it is an *example*, and in radical truth inhabited by singularities there is nothing like examples. But you do believe it, the poem then replies to itself with satanic paternosterical calm, because you are immune to disbelief. "Then his spirits declined . . ."[34]

What then is the radical thinking in Prynne, if its basis is neither realism and the mimesis of suffering and power, nor the rejection of realism and mimesis in pursuit of a more radical love? Prynne of course never defines radical thinking, nor does his poetry from *Brass* downward express much anxiety to be assimilated into any of the traditions of radical thinking on offer. Prynne's is not a partisan poetry and it is not an encrypted manifesto. John Wilkinson without fuss counts it as "radical poetry," but in several respects it appears to be plainly anti-radical.[35] The later poetry is split up with mockery of indistinct, hollow figures miming out a ventriloquism of the revolutionary phrase: prophetic souls at the garden party convention pressing forward to the barrier, as *Unanswering Rational Shore* singles them out in its doppelganger's non-identity parade.[36] This farce in the kodak gantry began in *Brass* and has not yet reached its credits. As early as the end of *The White Stones*, in 'As It Were An Attendant,' Prynne dismisses a "march | on the pentagon" as just another spin in "the prodigious cycle of ages." The revolutionary *événement* in this poem, a popular protest against American military power, flits by as *data* for a rhapsodic and inert structuralist anthropology, an academicism that pompously sees our contemporary proceedings and goings on—our "temporary nothing"—as evidently the modern guise of cyclical or sacred time.[37] The poem is more weary with structuralist anthropology and with phrases like "the cycle of ages" than it is interested in the march itself. Historical materialism, and its concept of developmental necessity in particular, are mocked as a crude résumé of authentic human historicity in the early poem 'Numbers in Time of Trouble.'[38] Alienation in Lukács's sense is scornfully abjured throughout Prynne's poetry, and most bluntly of all in the early poem 'Questions for the Time Being,' as an extortionate sentimental contrivance. Almost everything, snaps Prynne in hot reprimand of some projected subculturalist interlocutor, is surface; there is no "underground" for you to skulk into, the whole social plane is just ". . . the | mirror of a would-be alien who won't see how | much he is at home."[39] In a letter to Ed Dorn written during the period when he was at work on *The White Stones*, Prynne describes communism as "a sort of primal nostalgia," "a prelapsarian dialect, to describe the unattainable."[40] If Prynne's poetry is radical, it is not radical "Marxism."[41] But then, neither exactly is the *Contribution to the Critique of Hegel's Philosophy of Right*. Prynne's poetry, like that text, asks what size we are; it sometimes focuses attention on to its composition of that question, and at other times it thinks about what that question is and how to compose it without yet asking it or composing it.[42]

Radical thinking takes the size, measure or extent of the person as something that it alone must imperatively decide. To decide may mean to emphasise with new strength, to know by looking more closely or intently, or to restrict or aggrandize. It may mean representing subjectivity or persons in realistic terms, as it did for Lukács but not for Prynne. The question of size, in any case, is not just missing data for radical thinking. It is, in every case, a controversy.[43] Sometimes the question of size is the more or less formal, sometimes allegorical controversy that helps organise for radical thinking other seemingly less metaphysical and more political controversies, such as controversies to do with suffering, right or wealth. This is more or less what it is for Whitman, whose entire work is a radical, endless recomposition of the question of size answerable by song, by rhapsody and by the glorious contumacies of sexual passion. You are just as "immense and interminable" as these immense meadows and interminable rivers, sings Whitman to you; and—not *therefore* ("Down with causation," rejoins Olson) but *at the same time*—you are "Master or mistress in your own right over Nature."[44] But the question need not be in this way roughly allegorical, allowing the poet for example to commensurate personal amplitude and indivisibility with the political vindication of natural right. "Social architecture," wrote Mandelstam, "is measured against the scale of man."[45] What kind of measurement is this? For radical thinking, this common scale is not an *idea*, static and optional, nor is it simply a means of satire or the material for exhortation and panegyric, as it was for conservative thinkers like Dryden and Pound. The common scale is an *act* of radical recognition and understanding whose vocabulary of existential coordination is remade by every different measurement it yields; not, then, a "metaphor," but a work of difficult commensuration, the commensuration of person and world. What is "human," in Charles Tomlinson's words, "stands clarified | By all that accompanies and bounds."[46] This is a specific commensuration. To be bounded is to be illuminated and erect: I am a greater object because known more clearly and so *more* known. For the younger Prynne, as for the Tomlinson who influenced him, radical knowledge is always ontological augmentation: if I am more known, I know myself to be more.[47] I at the same time gain a world smaller by the measure of my augmentation, since the world must be intimate enough with my own single dimension to be the boundary of it.[48] To limit and bound, to be the extent, to be the term and definite resistance: this is the lexicon of the world's roles in Prynne's early poems and essays. When I know the world to be this small, *we* too are small: as Olson succinctly put it, and as Prynne certainly also believed before he wrote *Brass*, "It is not the many but the few who care | who keep alive what you set out to do."[49] We are small in ourselves ("We are | small / in the rain," says 'The Numbers'), and we who are small are small in number. We are small in number because through passion and intensity of insight we *know* that we must imperatively be what everyone truly is, though everyone may go on in this temporary nothing believing that he is something else, merely eating everyone instead of becoming their universal brother.[50] "The public," declares 'A Gold Ring Called Reluctance,' "is no more than a sign on the outside of the | shopping-bag; we are what it entails and | we remain its precondition."[51]

We who are small through the loss of illusion and the loss of self-estrangement are small in number: the few who care. This, as Prynne himself once said of the idea of unfixable performative self-fashioning in Frank O'Hara's 'In Memory of My Feelings,' is an American idea.[52] It is many other things besides, of course. *The White Stones* is a richly philological book, crammed and layered with knowledge often highly arcane and difficult of access (even in the new dawn of Google), with Biblical lamentation, Renaissance syncretistic cosmogony and a kind of sceptical, depsychologised Wordsworthian autobiography making up together the preponderance of literary allusion and influence. These are the traditions of thinking, text and utterance that Prynne acknowledges and keeps alive in his early poetry; but he keeps them alive so that he can bring their authority and their still living voices of anguish and exaltation to bear on the question of human size as lately reconstructed and propounded by Charles Olson. Olson's reconstruction is easy enough to dismiss as the atavistic persistence of "myth," or even as "gibberish," from the perspective of a latter-day criticism alert to all the gains to be made through sceptical deconstruction of the tropes, signifiers and image banks of enlightenment.[53] This work of critical exposure is important as well as easy enough. But just as important for an account of Prynne's writing is to understand how impressive and beautiful Olson's ideas were to him, and how those ideas commanded the thinking and imagination of someone who was, already in the late 1960s, at the very beginning of his writing life, a much greater poet than Olson ever was himself. I emphasise that these ideas were *beautiful* to Prynne; I think even that he loved them, and that he loved Olson for being the person who expressed them with such force as he did. I read Prynne's *Fire Lizard*, of which there is a hand made copy among Olson's letters from Prynne held at the University of Connecticut, bearing the inscription "For Charles, across the water, with love, New Year's Day 1970, Jeremy," as a last confession of that love—consciously the last Prynne would make.

Unless we can understand this, we will not see quite how difficult *Brass* was for Prynne, or be able to judge at what an immense and grievous expense of spirit he accomplished it; and if we underestimate that first and primary expense, we will mistake the whole course of Prynne's later work. Rather, then, than pointing out again, as has often been done, that Prynne broke with Olson in *Brass* and that this break was to be the onset of his mature work, we need first of all to follow what Olson said and what Prynne understood him to say. A longer account of that understanding will need to be offered elsewhere, but here at least is an outline. From here we can round on the question of Americanness.

Olson said that we must "find ways to stay in the human universe, and not to be led to partition reality at any point, in any way."[54] To stay in the largest world, in *das Diesseits* unsegregated into little lots and fates and unexpropriated of its native mythopoesis; to be the human immense enough to *be* that world and all its history; *we* must, imperatively, find ways to do this. We will find ways only if the human and the universal are held together in radical commensuration, and poetry is the language capable of making that bond of care. It may be and probably is the only language capable of it. Who then will be the person who makes this bond? In what figure of myself am I radically commensurable with the universe as a whole, and how within that figure must I begin to speak the poetic bond that commensurates us and that prepares us to be one and the same thing? Only man in his most immense figure, the figure whose suffering and whose exaltation are given a voice in Maximus, will make the universal human. He is, in Prynne's words, the cosmogenitor of "a lingual and temporal syncretism, poised to make a new order."[55] How are we, how is any one of us, to become this figure, the figure of maximum human amplitude? How is man to become the greatest object, the limit of the world and of history? He will become this figure first of all by being in the right place. The right place is the centre. From the centre of the world, I and the world are commensurable. In that commensuration achieved from the centre of the world, each of us, the world and I, will both magnify the other to its greatest dimension and diminish the other to the intimacy of truth. This will amount to more even than the "redefinition of the real" that was Melville's magnificent achievement;

it will make for us a real world transformed by "a secularization which
. . . loses nothing of the divine." This world is the "size man can once
more be capable of."[56] The intimacy of truth will be the intimacy of
this immense man's knowledge of any and every object. He will grasp
every object by the root. He will know in radical illumination

> that quality of any particular thing or event which comes in
> any one of our consciousnesses; how it comes in on us as a
> force peculiar to itself and to ourself in any of those instants
> which do hit us & of which our lives are made up. We call it
> size . . .[57]

Much of this thinking about what life in the world must be, and
what humans must do with language, given here only in the slightest
outline and so not yet fairly identifiable as "Olson's," is radical thinking.
It is, unquestionably, more "idealist" than "materialist," and it is, also
unquestionably, "ideology" in the sense given to that term by Marx's
and Engels's *The German Ideology*. It is also radical thinking. It is an
extremely rhapsodic radical thinking, spellbound in its own bravura
of utterance, perhaps incapable of conceiving any objects but the
greatest and the most infinitesimally particular; but for all its cognitive
paralyses it is what it describes objects to be, "a force peculiar to itself,"
compelling transformation of recognition by understanding and of
understanding by recognition, binding person and world together
into what Prynne in homage called "a width to be gauged | by the
most | specific & | hopeful | eye."[58]

For radical thinking, my life and the world, the life of any person
and the ensemble of social relations that Marx says she "is" in essence,[59]
must be commensurable here and now, whether or not my presence
in this world is central to it, and whether or not my knowledge and
perception of the world are creative of it, as Merleau-Ponty believed,
or, as Debord spectacularly urged, merely faced and fenced off by it.
Person and world are for radical thinking imperatively commensurable,
whether the object be the most alienated and diminutive onlooker or
the primogenitor of the whole universe: Gregor Samsa cringing in an
abyssally ordinary panic half under his bed, or Maximus of Gloucester,
the fundament all his own. In *The White Stones* Prynne acknowledges

both possibilities, each now flickering into view to confound the other by inflating or diminishing it. We are small and large, and the world is small and large; but this doubleness is not hailed by *The White Stones* with cosmic, Whitmaniacal indifference, it is mistrusted as a duplicity that cannot simply be confuted or ignored but must be outdone in a "prolonged action | of worked self-transcendence."[60] After that work, we are, because we must be, the "size [we] can once more be capable of." The world *could* then be "how far we | go, the practical limits of daylight," identical with our own movement in and through it and in that sense radically owned by us; it *could* be the great human "condition of landscape," described in 'First Notes on Daylight,' that spreads out from its centre in my own body, in all directions equally and at once, "like spokes from the nave of a wheel" whose distant "rim" is at once the visible horizon and the horizon of my knowledge, to use an image from Wordsworth's *Guide to the Lakes* that Prynne also uses in his poem 'Of Movement Towards a Natural Place.'[61] This central and immense body is our true size. A version of this body is described as in fact inalienable from us by Merleau-Ponty in 'Eye and Mind,' an article that Prynne described in a letter to Olson as "brilliant and marvellous." The immense body at the centre, Merleau-Ponty writes, "holds things in a circle round itself."[62] It is and I am—because it and I must be—as large as the circle that I hold. The circle is my tenacity. It is, in Prynne's phrase, my "own maximum."[63] The maximum is, if we open our eyes and grasp the world by the root, "the gauge of a life turning on the SINGLE CENTER."[64]

The White Stones tells us that we could be this man, that he is there for us in potential, if we will grasp him, that we might be (because we must be) the centre of the earth.[65] But it tells us also, even in its most hopefully rhapsodic poem, 'In Cimmerian Darkness,' that we have "long ignored" this man and "fervently refused" to be him, despite all our devout wishing;[66] and later still, in 'Crown,' nearer to the emphatic end of *The White Stones*, the book tells us, as though in extorted deference to some distastefully generic account of modern alienation, that our potentially transforming and radical trust is constricted "in the throat, in | the market-place," where Wordsworth's and Merleau-Ponty's great human wheel is pressed into work—by bathos—as a car steering wheel, an indifferent detail tossed into the dustbin of realism:"the faces dis- | owned by the shoes & overcoat settling in | behind the wheel and pulling the door shut."[67] *This*, writes Prynne, grimly lapsing from his usual sophistication with a stumping colon in 'Starvation / Dream,'"is not our planet: we have come | to the wrong place."[68]

That is of course not the end of it. Prynne does not abandon the question of size at the end of *The White Stones*, he says that we are the wrong size. He does not abandon it in *Brass*, he mocks his own former confidence in diagnosis of wrong from a still fiercer moral perspective.[69] He never abandoned the question of size and it never became for him any less imperative. What happens in Prynne's poetry, besides many other things, is that the question of size is again and again recomposed, typically in compressed, elliptical forms, presented indirectly and as connotation, or in one angle of a phrasal cluster, disintegrated from any shape of utterance that would allow us to acknowledge the question as such. The question will flash across the surface of a sentence that seems pointedly uninquisitive; or it will jut out as the unstable aggregate of words scattered across different points of a page whose echoes seem gripped into a semiotic concentration that is however unvoiceable. "[W]hy," Prynne asked in *The White Stones*, "should | the direct question not be put."[70] The direct question disappears from Prynne's poetry with *Brass*. Its last outing is in 'The Ideal Star-Fighter,' a masterpiece in every sense that is now unrepeatable in any of them:

> Yet how can we dream of
> the hope to continue, how can the vectors
> of digression not swing into that curve
> bounding the translocal, and slip over, so
> that the image of suffered love is
> scaled off, shattered to a granulated pathos
> like the dotted pigments of cygnus?
> (*Poems*, p.166)

This is the last direct question of size. There is almost another, but there is not one, one hundred and fifty-nine pages and twelve years later in *The Oval Window*: "You're flat out?"[71] The poem that asks this question, a question too diminutive and too blatantly an imported colloquialism to be what we know it is, ends with these lines:

> What else null else just else if before
> out into the garden with overshoot, the
> moon is bright as snowy day. In broad
> strip neon it ranks as a perfect crime.
>
> (*Poems*, p.325)

Close reading

This is what I mean by a question asked in aggregate, gripped into an unvoiceable semiotic concentration: it is the question of size, flaring in the absent italics of *overshoot* and *broad*, bouncing across the petty metrical compression of *What else etc*, towing the compliant lines home to their bathos. Radical illumination? Broad daylight—"how far we | go, the practical limits" of our human life in the truth of this world—is denied by enjambment belittled to a crude prank: not broad strip neon, even, but "broad | strip neon," even *this* insulting reality partitioned by its own poetic turn, the suspended adjective not really abused by what comes after it but confirmed in its uselessness for any other end. You're flat out? Want a raise?

> Hold one
>
> before leasing forage behaviour; wash the novice
> wrist, finger-tight. Do you already know this or yet
> allocate sufficiency.
>
> (*Poems*, p.554)

Do you already know it. If you do not know it yet, you may yet never know it; but if you do not yet "allocate sufficiency," that act by you is yet to come; and even in this obligatorily finical, discomposing summary of what the adverb "yet" presages, left as it is to the suspended last instant of a so-far direct question about to be broken off, the question of size is there as a frustration and a prevented hazard, the monosyllables too many and too crowded and in themselves too small, just as these clauses are too many and yet do not say enough: if you do not know it yet, you may yet never know it. What is this frustration of eloquence by its own particles *for*? Compression, distortion and aggregation of the question of size in Prynne's late work is not the textual equivalent of Freud's dream work, with some text or meaning in every case primed for interpretive recovery by a procedure of *Deutung* specially devised for it. The question is not a dream, it is a question in and about *this* world; it is not a question first for me as primary reader and then for me or someone else as later, technical reader, it is a question for *us* in the largest sense at our most wakeful, asked now and at any time with the same force and at all times equally intractable; and if the question cannot be understood in the form in which it is manifested in this poetry, that is because—well, why is that? Do you yet—because if you do not now, you for sure will at some time—allocate even to this incomplete and frustrated invocation of the question of size a sufficiency fit at least to snap the question shut and end it, ignoring for a moment, perhaps, in the remission of interpretive agitation granted by the full-stop, the complaint of your grammatical sense against the treatment of this too word-like "sufficiency" not as a quality of what has been allocated but as the direct object of allocation. Allocation then is malappropriation of the object; but grammar alone testifies to this, and grammar is everywhere else in this poem tensed and flouted (though never freely abandoned), so why should its distortion *here* count as a testimony of untruth or, at the very least, compel us into a routine of disbelief? Not, surely, for the simple reason that *here* is where *we* now are, and *our* grammar is still right? "Front match slides in tight . . ."[72]

Everywhere in Prynne's later poetry the question of size is *again* recomposed. Its compositions are such that it is difficult to understand what is being asked; but typically the force of the question will register no less strongly or injuriously for that. We can, if we like, back off slightly from the close reading of that one sentence from *Biting the Air* just attempted, "admit a little air now"[73] and remember our normal ways of talking about motive and interpretation. *Do you already know this or yet*—and then the discoordinating shift, the question cut and merged abruptly into an imperative: *allocate sufficiency*. In the face of this confrontation, why should the direct question not be put by a reader: why did Prynne do this? If he means to ask what size a person is, or what size I am, and also what size the world is, why should he compose these questions in forms that make them unaskable and leave them so strangely and improperly asked?

One answer, not the only one but an important one, runs as follows. After *Brass*, and because of it, the figure of Maximus grew for Prynne into a more and more diminutive answer to the question of size, more and more grisly with bathos. The figure of our "own maximum" is locked, most openly in *Wound Response* and *The Oval Window*, back into what Emerson called the "custody" of the private body and the "jail-yard of individual [political] relations" from which Olson had liberated him.[74] He becomes a joke figure, Gargantua of the homily and lectern, disowned by Prynne repetitively and with extreme semiotic, rhetorical, grammatical and satirical violence. We want him only with "lethal cupidity" and "limitless greed," and the love we are bribed into as consolation by his absence—*realism*—is "granulated pathos." "Do not love this man," barks the public health warning in 'The Bee Target on his Shoulder.' OK, the poem itself replies, I will match the definition of health, I will not love him; but, it then *later* says, "Love him, in *le silence des nuits, l'horreur des cimetières*."[75] I will make of him the dreamy object of a gothic prurience, not truly cutting off my greed for him altogether, but telling myself that the thin array and merely pleasant guise I fit him into is fantastical enough to guarantee venereal benignity. This is nothing but bathetic love as eupepsia, defecting regularly to pathos by the back door; and *Brass* despises whoever will grasp the maximum of man in this way merely by eating him. But the simple question remains: why is this gothic dream object what he becomes, why is this all that I can make of him, why must I therefore try forever and again and again to kill him by making the question unanswerable, *once I know that he is not what I am*?

At least since *Her Weasels Wild Returning*, Prynne's poetry has replied to this question with one answer which, though it might not often be direct and comprehensible, is nonetheless consistent. When I radically grasp this man who is, or who was once, or who must in truth be my "own maximum," he is not the root of the world. What is he then? In a word, he is imperialism. More specifically, he is American imperialism. Only a few will be, in Melville's words, "the man who, like Russia or the British Empire, declares himself a sovereign nature *olsen's attitude as an extension of American imperialism*

(in himself) amid the powers of heaven, hell, and earth."[76] The "size [we] can be once more be capable of" ceases to be for Prynne the amplitude of the person pervading and in magnificent harmony with the amplitude of the world. That idea is abruptly torn down by *Brass*, at the painful and perhaps even traumatic expense of real love for it, to reveal a wretched tangle of deceit and confabulation posing as radical commensuration; and "sovereign nature," that for Melville was so casually and proudly to be compared with imperialism, is discovered suddenly by Prynne in the deadlock of exactly that unbreakable connection, just at the moment when his poetry had drawn on all its most valuable resources of knowledge and passion to create the lyric song pledging our centrality to the world. To what world then has Prynne *already* pledged us as the centre? 'Chemins de Fer' turns this lyric song to bitter recantation:

> Even the thinnest breath of
> wind wraps round the intense lassitude, that
> an undeniably political centre keeps watch; the
> switch of light and shadow is packed with
> foreign tongues. I shall not know my own
> conjecture.
>
> (*Poems*, p.123)

Undeniability is not yet believability in *The White Stones*; but it will be yet. It will be more: we will be immune to disbelief, such that, perversely, and only perversely, denial is the stronger negation. No *polis*, but politics—and the grimness of that transition is that for Prynne, unlike for Pope, there is precisely nothing bathetic in what it leads to, but it makes bathos the superordinate linguistic mode of our continuity, the life of the language community then backwardly redefined as an ever-enlarged space for the retrogression of political and erotic emotion. What lies beyond that? "Without threat to its borders America was extending its empire," writes Robert von Hallberg. "Olson wanted a culture that could extend its power of explanation just as securely, effectively, and covertly."[77] And so it did. For us, now, this may be the easiest of observations both to make and to scorn. The imperialism of culture, the culture of imperialism, these are phrases we live with, the two words are just tied up, and Prynne's recent poetry knows better than any other poetry yet written that this kind of observation is easy for us and that these phrases are easy to live with. We do live with them. We live with them in fact so intelligently that the struggle to kill their ideological ancestors is not left to us. We know that the radical commensuration of man and world is a language game, or is ideology, or is the persistence as metaphor and cadential residue of the figurative language of religion, or is one aspect of the twisting mask of class and gender politics, just as Prynne knows it and says so; and we are right. Many poets know all this. But Prynne is the only poet in English whose language is permanently impacted not only by the truth of this intellectual disinheritance, but also by the *trauma* of its necessity. We all now rightly know enough not to be capable of radical love for ourselves and for the world grasped in one common bond together as the truth of intimacy and illimitability, and we are rightly eloquent enough not to be capable of speaking that bond as lyric poetry. Whoever might be the person capable of that act would be someone who did not live under capitalism, someone for whom the extension of economic ownership through imperial violence is not and cannot be the most radical form of self-extension; and as we know, since we know enough, and since we eat enough, living under capitalism is not itself an act anyone can desist from, terminate, or even pause in. Try doing it now.

NOTES

[1] J.H. Prynne, 'First Notes on Daylight,' *Poems*. Tarset: Bloodaxe Books, 2005: 69.

[2] 'Shortly delude berries in a pot,' *Red D Gypsum, Poems*: 441.

[3] Marx, *A Contribution to the Critique of Hegel's Philosophy of Right*. Introduction. In *Early Writings*. Trans. Rodney Livingstone and Gregor Benton. New York: Vintage, 1975: 244, 251. "Mensch, das ist kein abstraktes, außer der Welt hockendes Wesen. Der Mensch, das ist die Welt des Menschen, Staat, Sozietät." "Radikal sein ist die Sache an der Wurzel fassen. Die Wurzel für den Menschen ist aber der Mensch selbst." *Die Frühschriften*. Ed. Siegfried Landshut. Stuttgart: Alfred Kröner, 1971:

208, 216.

4 One real alternative is Kant. Kant's term translated as "cognitive faculties" is *Erkenntnisvermögen*. Paul Guyer and Allen Wood point out that Vermögen "implies activity," and that, for Kant, even "our senses are acted upon by external objects;" but the activity and passivity of cognitive faculties in Kant is transcendentally determined, fixedly systematic and not reciprocally transformative. 'Introduction,' Immanuel Kant, *Critique of Pure Reason*. Trans. and ed. Paul Guyer and Allen W. Wood. Cambridge: Cambridge University Press, 1997: 39.

5 *Early Writings*: 244; *Frühschriften*: 209.

6 Examine in homeopathic isolation Prynne's poem 'Select an object with no predecessors,' in *For The Monogram*, *Poems*: 420. Could this be what Hans Thill and Ulf Stolterfoht call "Prynne's language of Paradise," the "complete dehierarchization of the structure of syntax" that would presumably outlaw bathos from sentence structure? See their 'Nachwort,' J.H. Prynne, *Poems | Gedichte*. Trans Ulf Stolterfoht and Hans Thill. Heidelberg: Wunderhorn, 2007: 73.

7 Heidegger, *Being and Time*. Trans. John Macquarrie and Edward Robinson. Oxford: Blackwell, 1962: 195: "What is decisive is not to get out of the circle but to come into it in the right way ... In the circle is hidden a positive possibility of the most primordial kind of knowing." Prynne, "We inserted our names would we sing," *Word Order*, *Poems*: 360. Cf. *Unanswering Rational Shore*, 527: "indistinctly invited into the loop."

8 *Early Writings*: 244; *Frühschriften*: 209.

9 The modicum of Leibnizian theodicy in the raw in this thinking from 1843-4 is later cooked up, in a highly literary footnote in *Capital*, into an outright satire on "the trite ideas held by the self-complacent bourgeoisie with regard to their own world, to them the best of all possible worlds." Karl Marx, *Capital*. Ed. Friedrich Engels, rev. Ernest Untermann, trans. Samuel Moore and Edward Aveling. New York: Modern Library, 1936: 93.

10 *Early Writings*: 244; *Frühschriften*: 209.

11 Ibid.

12 'The Ideal Star-Fighter,' *Poems*: 166.

13 This relationship of radical thinking to its object was identified and condemned by John Dryden in his preface to *Religio Laici*. Dryden concludes the preface, which is a conservative attack on Deists and other recusants who dare "offend Infinity," by denouncing precisely this "fanatique" habit of arguing: "The Expressions of a Poem, design'd purely for Instruction, ought to be Plain and Natural, and yet Majestick: for here the Poet is presum'd to be a kind of Law-giver, and

those three qualities which I have nam'd are proper to the Legislative style. The Florid, Elevated and Figurative way is for the Passions; for Love and Hatred, Fear and Anger, are begotten in the Soul by shewing their Objects out of their true proportion; either greater than the Life, or less; but Instruction is to be given by shewing them what they naturally are. A Man is to be cheated into Passion, but to be reason'd into Truth." See ll.92-98 for a grotesque sketch of the "rebell" thinker as a "poor Worm" who thinks he himself is justice. *The Poems and Fables of John Dryden.* Ed. James Kinsley. London: Oxford UP, 1962: 282, 284. Cf. Richard Rorty's consanguine dismissal of radical thinking of the "Sartrean or Savonarolan sort" as "the quest for purity of thought . . . gone rancid": "It is the attempt to see yourself as an incarnation of something larger than yourself (the Movement, Reason, the Good, the Holy) rather than accepting your finitude." *Philosophy and Social Hope.* London: Penguin,1999: 13.

¹⁴ *Poems*: 10–11.

¹⁵ From the second formal lesson of *Kitchen Poems*, 'Die A Millionaire,' Poems: 13. *Kitchen Poems* might usefully be compared with W.S. Graham's 'Johann Joachim Quantz's Five Lessons' from his 1977 collection *Implements In Their Places.* The poems are not similar, but the contrast points up how much of the quality of thinking in Prynne's 1968 book is owed to his early strong antipathy to "dramatic monologue." W.S. Graham, *New Collected Poems.* Ed. Matthew Francis. London: Faber, 2004: 228–31. There is almost a parody of dramatic monologue and the tedious virtue it makes of "mimesis" in Prynne's 'One Way At Any Time,' *Poems*: 110: "The girl | leans over to clear off my plate, hey I've not | finished yet, the man opposite without think- | ing says must be on piecework and" etc.

¹⁶ Compare Friedrich Schlegel's *Lucinde and the Fragments.* Trans. Peter Firchow. Minneapolis: University of Minnesota Press, 1971: 256: "All self-sufficiency is radical, is original, and all originality is moral, is originality of the whole man. Without originality, there is no energy of reason and no beauty of disposition." For an immensely thorough and penetrating examination of the concept of autonomy (especially in psychoanalytic thinking), see Matthew ffytche, "'The Most Obscure Problem Of All": Autonomy and its Vicissitudes in The Interpretation of Dreams,' *Psychoanalysis and History* 9(1) (2007): 39–70.

¹⁷ In other words, to borrow Etienne Balibar's phrase, Marx is a philosopher and "philosophy is a practice of writing." Eva L. Corredor, *Lukács After Communism. Interviews With Contemporary Intellectuals.* Durham and london: Duke UP, 1997: 116. Not just fundamentalists but literary critics,

too, persist in regarding Marx as something other than a writer. See for example Mutlu Konuk Blasing, *Lyric Poetry. The Pain and the Pleasure of Words*. Princeton: Princeton University Press, 2007: 3–4, where everything Marx wrote after his juvenile poems is discovered to be "disciplinary discourse" which "must rule out and/or censor poetry" and which "inaugurates itself as 'not poetry'." Friedrich Schlegel overruled this finicality a couple of centuries in advance in *Literary notebooks, 1797–1801*. Ed. Hans Eichner. London: Athlone, 1957: 21: "All prose is poetic."

[18] For Judith Butler, *Gender Trouble. Feminism and the Subversion of Identity*. New York: Routledge, 2006 we will often find that what we unthinkingly hold to be facts impervious to epistemic regime change are nothing but "regulatory fiction" disciplining thought (33), and that even the features of a person's identity most compellingly recognised by intuition are not truly foundations but are "foundational illusions of identity" that need imperatively to be cut back, diminished in authority, deflated by critique (46). Butler's radical feminist criticism of the discourses of identity is in this respect like Marx's critique of religion, in that, like Marx, she makes the object of radical thinking, in this case not *der Mensch* but "identity," both smaller and greater than it is for the thinking she means to oppose. Smaller because stripped of its great aegis of heteronormative presuppositions and illusions, greater because thereby liberated into the dimension of performativity unconstricted by foundationalist ontology.

[19] As asserted by, amongst others, John Wilkinson, *The Lyric Touch*. Great Wilbraham: Salt, 2007: 121.

[20] 'Refuse Collection,' *Quid* 13: IRA QUID (2004) [n.p.]; *To Pollen*. London: Barque, 2006: 21. The skid of 'Refuse Collection' is punctuated by blank lines separating apparently discrete sections of lyric. The visual reference (another layer of crudity and grotesque) is to Wordsworth whose typographical practice this was, and whose "self-possession felt in every pause," *The Prelude* (1805) IV. 398 is re-uptaken at the end of Prynne's poem and replaced by "the wanton ambit of self possession."

[21] Jennifer Cooke, 'Warring Inscriptions: J.H. Prynne's To Pollen,' http://intercapillaryspace.blogspot.com/2007/04/warring-inscriptions-j-h-prynnes-to.html describes how this text teaches readers "to be suspicious of the desire for translucency" aroused by its own complexity.

[22] *Poems*: 414. On the Gulf War as the subject of 'Weasels', see Keston Sutherland, 'Ethica Nullius,' *Avant-Post: The Avant-Garde Under "post-" Conditions*. Ed. Louis Armand. Prague: Literaria Pragensia, 2006: 239–55.

[23] 'Foaming metal sits not far in front,' in *Not-You, Poems*: 385. This poem is

another of Prynne's tractates on what Samuel Beckett, *Watt*. London:
John Calder, 1976: 156 called the "hideous . . . semi-colon."

[24] *Poems*: 162. For an extended commentary on 'L'Extase de M. Poher,' see
Keston Sutherland, *J.H. Prynne and Philology*. Cambridge: Unpublished
PhD dissertation, 2004: Ch.5.

[25] 'What then hunger to a first date peckish on ready,' in *Biting The Air*,
Poems: 555.

[26] Theodor Adorno, *Negative Dialektik. Jargon der Eigentlichkeit*. Frankfurt
am Main: Suhrkamp, 2003: 29; *Negative Dialectics*. Trans. E.B. Ashton.
London: Routledge, 1990: 17–18.

[27] 'The Ideal Star-Fighter,' *Poems*: 165.

[28] 'Slick film so crested in white reward,' in *Pearls That Were*, *Poems*: 456. The
epigraph is Ibid. 311.

[29] Poems: 82–3, 103. *The White Stones* would not accept the name "autobiography." Its alternative is mounted at the conclusion of 'The Com-
mon Gain, Reverted': "As I walked up the hill this evening and felt |
the rise bend up gently against me I knew | that the void was gripped
with concentration. | Not mine indeed but the sequence of fact, | the
lives spread out . . ." Ibid.: 89. The use of traditional metre here thickens the claim to impersonality.

[30] Ibid.: 77.

[31] Ibid.: 23.

[32] Ibid.: 166.

[33] See *Pearls That Were*, *Poems*: 464: "As to go for a dancer in yellow, | for to
dance to the far brim, | all in yellow, all in yellow sliding | and ready
to come in."

[34] Ibid.: 167.

[35] John Wilkinson, *The Lyric Touch*: 26. Elsewhere (115) Wilkinson fits the
phrase with scare quotes, but again without specifying what it means
or why it doesn't.

[36] *Poems*: 530. Hollow humanity in Prynne is of course not the target for
brunts of lamentation that it is for Eliot. It is zero pathos.

[37] Ibid.: 124. The "temporary nothing in which life goes on" is the last
twist of 'Questions for the Time Being,' Ibid: 113. On sacred time,
see Mircea Eliade, *Le mythe de l'éternel retour*. Paris: Gallimard, 1949.
Prynne mentioned reading Eliade in a letter to Olson, 17th April 1964.
Prynne's letters are quoted throughout this article by permission of
The University of Connecticut at Storrs.

[38] *Poems*: 17. Prynne dislikes the idea of "entailment," on grounds that seem
to have as much to do with etymology as with politics. "[W]rong," so
the poem tells us, "follows into the glowing tail of "history" as | for

example the Marxist comet burns with | such lovely, flaring destruc-
tion."

[39] Ibid.: 112. To reject the Lukács of *History and Class Consciousness* so sum-
marily is, as Axel Honneth and many others have implied, more or less
to reject at its root the whole tradition of "Western Marxism." Axel
Honneth, *Verdinglichung. Eine anerkennungstheoretische Studie*. Frankfurt
am Main: Suhrkamp, 2005: 11–12. Of course, how much we are at
home is a question to which *The White Stones* makes no definite answer:
the would-be alien won't see, but we ought-to-be domestics very often
can't see.

[40] Letter to Dorn, 26th July 1964. The previous month Prynne had asked,
in revolted response to pro-Vietnam war U.S. journalism, "emotionally
how can anyone help being a near-Marxist." Letter to Olson, 25th June
1964. Whatever Prynne at this point thought anyone ought to be, he
clearly did not think that he ought to be it "emotionally."

[41] As David Marriott, *An Introduction to the Poetry of J.H. Prynne* (1962–1977).
Unpublished DPhil dissertation: University of Sussex, 1993: 157
observed: "for Prynne, historical shifts in substance are based on the
ruptural effects of qualitative process and not on the Marxian crux of
technologies and historical materialism."

[42] Unlike Marx's text, however, Prynne's poetry does not state at all clearly
that, in Marx's words, "the weapon of criticism cannot replace the criticism of weapons, and material force must be overthrown by material
force," though 'The Ideal Star-Fighter,' *Poems*: 166 does ridicule mere
"moral stand-by" as "no substitute for 24-inch | reinforced concrete."
Marx's early obsession with chiasmus and rhetorical inversion in this instance muddies the argument it makes, as "Kritik der Waffen" might be
misunderstood by pacifistically gentle readers to mean only "criticism
directed against weapons," whereas of course it also (and primarily)
means "criticism carried out with the use of weapons." *Early Writings*.
251; *Frühschriften*: 216. For a commentary on "the idea of measure" in
one early poem by Prynne, see Alizon Brunning and Robin Purves,
'Smaller Than The Radius Of The Planet', *Quid 17: For J.H. Prynne*
(Summer, 2006): 15–18. N.H. Reeve and Richard Kerridge, *Nearly Too
Much: The Poetry of J.H. Prynne*. Liverpool: Liverpool University Press,
1995: 1–36 discuss "questions of scale," but these are questions to do
with the perception and description of large and small physical processes and the effect of language switching between them, not with the
size of the person and the world. These switchings can be "radically
disruptive of the self," Reeve and Kerridge argue; but they do not say
what makes this disruption "radical," what "the self" is that is vulnerable

to radical disruption, what happens to the self thus radically disrupted or, perhaps most importantly, why Prynne should want to inflict radical disruption on a self vulnerable to it.

[43] Hume describes the "dispute, concerning the dignity or meanness of human nature" as a "controversy" that is often more "verbal" than "real." I borrow his term "controversy" in homage to this observation, but would add, as Hume does not, that the elimination of so-called verbal controversy by reduction of the terms of argument to a common language is itself politically controversial. What Hume calls "verbal controversy" capable of an agreeable restatement might really be a disagreement in consciously and conspicuously tendentious terms. There are problems that would lose their imperative form and so be deradicalised if the language in which they are stated were agreeable and capable of determination by common consensus. The fact that thought can be deradicalised by language does not strike Hume as a cause for anxiety, nor does it seem to him to have anything really to do with thought. The reason for this is of course that Hume wants to have language at his disposal as a means to deradicalise thought whose radicalism he dislikes. David Hume, 'Of the Dignity or Meanness of Human Nature,' *Essays Moral, Political and Literary*. Ed. Eugene F. Miller. Indianapolis: Liberty Fund, 1985: 81.

[44] Walt Whitman, 'To You,' ll.41, 43. *The Complete Poems*. Ed. Francis Murphy. London: Penguin, 1996: 263–4. Charles Olson, 'The Present is Prologue,' *Collected Prose*. Ed. Donald Allen and Ben Friedlander. Berkeley: University of California Press, 1997: 205. Notice that Whitman here writes "meadows and rivers" and not, say, "continents and oceans." This is not bathos. There is no bathos in Whitman's universe, first, because every object is cosmic and cosmogenic, and second, because there is no neoclassicism to reduplicate the distinctions of class.

[45] Osip Mandelstam, 'Humanism and the Present,' *The Collected Critical Prose and Letters*. Ed. Jane Gary Harris. Trans. Jane Gary Harris and Constance Link. London: Collins Harvill, 1991: 181.

[46] Charles Tomlinson, 'At Delft,' *Collected Poems*. Oxford: Oxford University Press, 1985: 32.

[47] On the influence of Tomlinson on Prynne (via Donald Davie) in the early 1960s, see Keston Sutherland, *J.H. Prynne and Philology*: 115–125. Prynne admired Tomlinson's *Seeing is Believing*. London: Oxford UP, 1960, but criticised it in terms of the question of size, arguing that it is open only "to certain narrowly specific features of the known world" and incapable of meeting "the pressure of a personal or social milieu." Letter to Ed Dorn, 9th July 1962.

[48] Olson tried to literalise this thought in 'Human Universe,' *Collected Prose:* 161: "the skin itself, the meeting edge of man and external reality, is where all that matters does happen, that man and external reality are so involved with one another that, for man's purposes, they had better be taken as one." Prynne tries to repeat this literalisation in 'The Numbers,' *Poems:* 10, but is already a good enough poet to mangle the idea, without meaning to, through decorative and inert syntactic disruption.

[49] Charles Olson, *The Maximus Poems.* Ed. George F. Butterick. Berkeley: University of California Press, 1983: 22.

[50] *Poems:* 10.

[51] Ibid.: 22.

[52] 'Poetry and Language' lecture series, University of Cambridge, 25th February 2003. Prynne concluded his discussion of 'In Memory of My Feelings' with the remark: "if I were living in Baghdad now I would not be prepared to read a poem like this."

[53] On "myth": Anthony Mellors, *Late Modernist Poetics from Pound to Prynne.* Manchester: Manchester University Press, 2005. On "gibberish:" David Marriott, *An Introduction to the Poetry of J.H. Prynne:* 143.

[54] Charles Olson, 'Human Universe,' *Collected Prose:* 157.

[55] J.H. Prynne, 'Charles Olson, Maximus Poems IV,V,VI,' *The Park* 4/5 (Summer 1969): 64-66. Reprinted in *Io* 16 (Winter 1972–73): 89-92.

[56] Charles Olson, 'Equal, That Is, to the Real Itself,' *Collected Prose:* 120; 'Proprioception,' Ibid. 190; 'The Gate and the Center,' Ibid. 172.

[57] 'The Materials and Weights of Herman Melville,' Ibid. 117.

[58] 'Fri 13,' *Poems:* 50.

[59] Marx, sixth thesis on Feuerbach, *Early Writings:* 423.

[60] *Poems:* 113. Kevin Nolan, 'Capital Calves: Undertaking an Overview,' *Jacket* 24 (2003) http://jacketmagazine.com/24/nolan.html mistakes this for "an Eliotic dream," but for Prynne self-transcendence was emphatically not deliverance into any climacteric that passeth understanding.

[61] "Only at the rim does the day tremble and shine." *Poems:* 223. This line is quoted by Ed Dorn, verbatim except for a rather dazzlingly illustrative line break after "rim" and a still-Olsonian ampersand in place of the word "and," in Book IV of *Gunslinger.* Durham, NC: Duke UP, 1989: 147. William Wordsworth, *Guide to the Lakes.* Ed. Ernest de Sélincourt. London: Frances Lincoln, 2004: 42.

[62] Maurice Merleau-Ponty, *L'Œil et l'Esprit.* Paris: Gallimard, 1964: 19; 'Eye and Mind,' trans. Carleton Dallery, *The Primacy of Perception.* Ed. James M. Edie. Evanston: Northwestern University Press, 163. Merleau-Ponty's phrase is highly metrical, virtually an iambic pentameter: "il tient

les choses en cercle autour de soi." This must have sharpened its impact on Prynne, who urged Olson to read the article in a letter dated 6th March, 1964.

[63] 'The Corn Burned by Syrius,' *Poems*: 126.

[64] Charles Olson, 'The Gate and the Center,' *Collected Prose*: 171.

[65] The importance of cosmogenic centrality in Prynne's work is discussed at length in Keston Sutherland, 'Ethica Nullius.' The radical thinking of Pico della Mirandola discussed in that essay is echoed across the centuries by Friedrich Schlegel, *Kritische Schriften und Fragmente*. Ed. Ernst Behler and Hans Eichner. Paderborn: Schöningh, 1988 vol.2: 230: "We will know man when we know the centre of the earth."

[66] *Poems*: 75. Wishing is invariably an inadequate or misguided act in the existential lexicon of Prynne's early work. The wish expressed in 'Charm Against Too Many Apples' is faintly petulant, or in any case it is a hurried form of desiring. *Brass* batters the wish in caustics and serves it with newspaper and no chips in 'A New Tax on the Counter-Earth:' "A dream in sepia and eau-de-nil ascends | from the ground as a great wish for calm." In the wake of May 1968 and the Israeli-Egyptian war of 1967–70, wishing is Nile water puffed through the vaporizer of the unconscious. Ibid.: 68, 172. Prynne's hostility to wishing is part of his early and persistent distrust of Freudian theory, which begins to emerge as adamant creed and stricture in 'Star Damage at Home' ("I will not be led | by the mean- | ing of my | tinsel past or | this fecund hint | I merely live in") and comes fully into the open as sarcastic dismissal in 'L'Extase de M. Poher' ("what person could be generalised | on a basis of "specifically" sexual damage, | the townscape of that question." This is "Freudian history," the bathos of ontology). Ibid.: 109, 161. For an extended commentary on 'L'Extase de M. Poher,' see Keston Sutherland, *J.H. Prynne and Philology*. Cambridge: Unpublished PhD dissertation, 2004: Ch.5.

[67] *Poems*: 116. I say that the *The White Stones* has an emphatic end, and this is true especially of the run of poems from 'Starvation / Dream' onward, all of which are bitterly self-terminating (with the exception of 'Smaller than the Radius of the Planet,' which belongs at the end of the book mainly on the strength of its two virgules and the gritted medial hiatus in its 11th line); but the most terminal end on offer to Prynne was not chosen by him: he did not end with the grievous mostlys and faded retrograde ampersands of 'As It Were An Attendant,' but instead with the still-working, intractable intellectual pathos of 'The Corn Burned by Syrius.'

[68] Ibid.: 114.

[69] I have avoided using the word "dialectic" in this essay, partly because I fear that its appearance here would have encouraged a lazy reading of my argument by anyone who thinks that he already knows what the word means (which of course anyone very well may), and more importantly because I hope to make readers feel the necessity of dialectical thinking by feeling how problematic is the absence of any direct treatment of it. In any case, if I had used the word, I would have used it at this moment.

[70] 'Questions for the Time Being,' *Poems*: 112.

[71] Ibid.: 325.

[72] 'We'll mark them out,' *Poems*: 448. Peter Middleton, 'Distant Reading'. *Performance, Readership, and Consumption in Contemporary Poetry*. Tuscaloosa: University of Alabama Press, 2005: 176, prejudges the question I'm setting up here by referring to "excess semantic complexity" in Prynne's late poetry. Excess to what measure of requirement, for what extent of person, in how large a world? Excessive for a slide in brief? 'Her Weasels Wild Returning', *Poems*: 411.

[73] 'We'll mark them out,' Ibid.: 448.

[74] Ralph Waldo Emerson, *Essays and Lectures*. New York: The Library of America, 1983: 460.

[75] *Poems*: 150–2.

[76] Herman Melville, Letter to Nathaniel Hawthorne, 1851. *Correspondence*. Ed. Lynn Harth. Evanston: Northwestern UP, 1993: 186.

[77] Robert von Hallberg, *Charles Olson. The Scholar's Art*. Cambridge, Mass.: Harvard University Press, 1978: 28.

MANY VOICES: *SINGING*

John Douglas Templeton

I discovered J.H. Prynne in a library: an appropriate setting in which to uncover work that was itself became such a hugely diverse source of ideas & inspirations. It was from a speculative position of total ignorance that I first opened that 'yellow brick', the collected *Poems* from Bloodaxe. On the pages I found an abundance of something completely fresh. A way of presenting words that I had never before encountered. Then, as I read these fragmented words, I discovered poetry with a luminous intensity of tone. An exciting bafflement crossed my mind which intrigued me & sent me home with the book. I was beginning my study of composition at the time. I was hungry for the influence of new voices which could contribute to my music. Prynne's work has been such an influence for me and has inspired several of my own musical works into which I have incorporated the texts. The poems have been both springboards to inspire new projects and prisms to help to attune existing ideas. I have always read these poems unguided and have built a personal response to them from only my own reactions. From the poems I have derived a set of technical musical devices which have fed into my musical language. And as my musical language developed alongside my unfolding attitudes Prynne's poems the body of work itself has provided encouragement in prizing a constantly inventive course. There seems always to be a temptation, as I make work, to bend towards a normalizing influence, to regress to an easier and more banal route. But Prynne's output has always seemed to me to be a justification for resisting the forces of the ordinary and banal in favour of the more difficult road of invention.

Prynne, the man himself and his reputation, was unknown to me when I began reading his poems. It was only later that I discovered that this poetry was supposed to be difficult. Of course, the poems seemed instantly rather different to the hegemonic mass of poems available to a casual observer such as I: the mainstream. Read without the prejudice of prior knowledge it was only later that I uncovered a faint suspicion. The suspicion was really against work which moves towards the boundaries of normal meaning, ordinary poetic discourse. These poems are so entirely different from mainstream poetry in this way because they prioritize different aspects of language and words. I am not a poet and I am certainly no scholar of English Literature. I was not lucky enough to be introduced to modern poetry at school. Even at university I have found very few people aware of the work going on in contemporary poetry. In this world there are no recognizable situations from everyday life, everyday grammar, everyday words. I was not discouraged from this work by its seeming unintelligibility only because I recognized this from my musical appreciation. I was, on the contrary, captivated and astonished by such a manifest complexity and found these unusual creations rich with possibility. They put ambiguity in the foreground and achieve an authenticity by acknowledging the dangerous spaces in language. There is something about the voice of these poems which led me to trust the author. I felt sure that I could rely on the writer's decisions. After all, the poems seemed to me undoubtedly beautiful. And even if I could not instantly understand them I had the instinctive feeling that deep meaning lay wrapped in the poems. I suspect that there is also a more explicit relationship, at a deep and significant level, between the reading a Prynne poem and listening to a piece of music.

When my exploration brought me in contact with Prynne I was fairly new to the creative impulse. A composer writing music now has to make many decisions about his identity and it is difficult to find a position on the artistic spectrum. To choose to create is difficult. This is not the path of least resistance and represents a leap into unknown and often ambiguous areas. It came as a massive relief to me to discover that a world of modernism existed at all in poetry. There can be no doubting that modernism can have tendency to be baffling. Prynne's poems I found an actually very approachable form of modernism. It is made approachable through the great conviction and focus of its many voices and the the appealing fecundity of invention in all spheres: vocabulary & rhythm; images & structure. The poems are so often joyous, acerbic and startling. They are strong tracts as much as they are tender love lyrics. I can vividly remember first grappling with *Fire Lizard*. I was trying to make this into a piece and trying to 'analyze' the poem. At some point something snapped and I realized that their was a direct voice coming through the poem. It was a singing voice, like a *cantus firmus* embedded in the poem. I stopped trying to slice the poem up and started 'hearing' it.

As a non-expert reader of Prynne I would say that I have a certain ritualized behavior with the poems. When I come to read a poem I firstly must read through from beginning to end. This first reading, like many further readings, is a sort of sieved understanding. As I read I filter. There are usually many words whose meaning I do not know. If I skip these and keep going I allow myself to glimpse the overall shape, the rhythmic and lyrical flow of the whole poem. Then I will make some research into the poem's content. This is usually the dictionary first and perhaps an encyclopedia or the internet. It is with no embarrassment that I admit that in my first journey through the poem I am sometimes completely bamboozled by the literal meanings of the majority of the words and concepts. Nevertheless, I think it is important to, not ignore, but to file these problems away for later. So each time I do a little research and reread the poem some new parts of the work are illuminated. There form little constellations of significance around certain words or phrases which become attached to the arch of my first reading. And as such each reading is a development. This process goes on and on and there is not a single poem where I could reach a conclusion. This is so pertinent to the way musical structures are conceived. Conductors in first rehearsals will often demand a complete run of a piece from the beginning to the conclusion, despite problems which emerge on the way, because it is so important to understand where each moment fits into a musical whole. So too with these poems it is so important, I feel, to feel the unfolding arc, and to consider the contribution of each word to the whole trajectory. This, if grasped, can help to calm those worries of 'not understanding.'

In their vast variance Prynne's poems form a sort of source book of invention and intrigue. Throughout my early compositions I was always searching for those sources which could help inspire new work and engender confidence to follow a rather vague path: an idealistic path of modernism, newness, profundity and chaos which I had in some corner of my mind. I think that composers, and perhaps artists of all kinds, search in the other media for ideas and approaches in order to will shed light indirectly on their own creative processes. There is also a specific necessity for those composers who are interested in making music for the human voice to find poets who create work which can be integrated into his personal style. I have always been interested in the often uneasy relationship between music and words. Despite the difficulties of integrating two media poetic text of some kind is usually necessary to activate the human voice. A singer's musical paths are always modulated through words or phonemes in some specific pattern. So composers are always searching for poets and always seemingly finding it problematic. It has always surprised me that composers, including many of those whose aim is to develop a highly sophisticated modern language, will, when turning to write vocal music, employ a text which is in itself old-fashioned and conservative. It is not perhaps essential for all composers to find a text which mirrors in ambition that of the music but, for me it was a natural step. This is not to deny the straightforward 'magic' of inspiration. It is clear that 'Now if you step down into starlight . . .' ('A Night Square') will engender a different sort of singing from 'The prism crystal sets towards the axis of episodic desire.' ('Chromatin') Even aside from the technical problems associated with setting the word 'prism' for a singer (just try it!) the former phrase is suggestive of an expansive lyric quality, an openness of vowel and a certain smoothness where the later has a jerky sparkle and a much more energized layer of consonants.

My explorations into poetry have been random and directionless beginning as they did from a state of almost total ignorance. Most of this high modernism from the early parts of the twentieth century is off-putting to the under educated reader. It seems formidably leaned and scholarly. I know nothing of Greek, Latin and the Classics. I am unlikely to spot allusions to great works of literature and am particularly unlikely to garner much enlightenment from unfamiliar foreign languages. I was deeply intimidated by these masters who can appear willfully obscure. But the Prynne seems to me to be instantly much less cerebral and scholarly because the music sings through. Singing not only with fluid lyricism but also modern melodies, like Olivier Messiaen's, leaping in bold directions: unusual and angular. And a rhythmic impulsion which matches the riotous scores of Stravinsky. These are poems which grip the reader in an energetic process. These are not poems stiffened by their own intelligence into an over-learned stasis. It was through Prynne's poems that I then found a strategy for reading other poems which I had previously been too scared to attempt. It gave me the confidence, in some ways, to approach these poems with my own agenda and not to worry about 'finding the *correct* answer.' A significant bonus to my discovery of Prynne was that it empowered me to go back to these tough early modernists with a new.

When instructing a singer to perform a word, or a phrase or an entire poem there are many choices. A word may be declaimed in such a way that the audience can hear it. Or, it may be obscured to varying degrees, by lengthening the time over which the word in uttered, by obscuring the voice under the sound of instruments, or by separating the syllables of the word to extreme distances. These techniques are all in the gamut of the composer and a thorough use of these begin to change the poem. So writing music with a poem is a useful way to gain access to the poem itself. I have often reached the end of the composition process, with a completed piece in my hands, and wished I could back and do the whole thing again. Start at the beginning and retake all the decisions under the light of what I have learned. Perhaps I will, one day. But I feel it is in the spirit of Prynne to embrace this grappling. There are all those 'loopholes' which we will never be able to control. And thank goodness for that.

Music does not, other than in the limited sphere of sound-effects, relate by a significant relationship to the sounds of the 'real world'. As a composer I will always be attracted to the abstract side of any artwork. Prynne's work is so appealing in the fact that it puts such abstract considerations in the foreground. He does this without, however, sterilizing the quality of invention. The amount of invention is prolific in these poems and it is not hampered by formal considerations: it is heightened by them. I sometimes feel that the poems have an organic life in themselves which I am watching and experiencing as it unfolds over the course of the poems. The poetic text always seems to be in discourse with a hidden level of creative force. The interaction of form and content is like the explosive growth of bacteria within a rigid cage. Sometimes I feel that the outcome of a particular poem is in jeopardy as it moves, turbulently, through its many strange landscapes.

A musical discourse is one that makes its arguments from sound alone. It is in the structures and forms of music that we locate meaning. Many link music to language & there are important similarities. They are declaimed directly to the audience: a piece of music directs itself towards the listener as a poem addresses a reader, both as an individual and as part of a greater collective audience. But music is never literal in the way that words can appear to be. Before discovering Prynne dissatisfaction with this poetic literalism consistently discouraged me. Words will always signify some real thing but the contexts of Prynne's poems liberate them from that rather pedestrian level of meaning and stretch them up into the sky.

Prynne's poems were the first to show me that there could be a different mode of meaning. This was a different significance in the text which was more closely related to the modes of meaning in music. Here it became clear that words do not mean as words might mean in conversation, in storytelling, in documentary. The words mean in relation to each other, in the patterns and ripples they make through time. Not just in reference outward to the worlds of physical things & our experiences. Not only those things but very forcefully in relation to the context which is gradually unfolded as the poem progresses & this is rather as the notes and sound-gestures of a musical work relate to each other. Music is often spoken of as a language. Often it seems to be some kind of overheard language of another species where we can only guess at the significance of the utterances.

Since discovering these strange poems in the library I have written a quartet of pieces taking influence directly form Prynne's poems: 'Fire Lizard', a string quartet with baritone; 'Night Square', an opera; 'the whole cloud is bright & assembled now', for orchestra; & most recently 'Chromatin' for tenor and ensemble. These poems have a flexibility of construction. The edges can take many forms. The boundaries between the parts of writing can be blurred in such a way that ordinary words and phrases become enjoined in strange ways. The glue of the language has been allowed to melt away and seepage can occur creating lines of poetry that elude capture. It becomes impossible to pin the poem down. It moves around as you try to read it because the workings of the text are manifold. Text like this is seemingly far more energetic that the poems I had read before. The atrophic boundaries of these poems are close to the shifting landscapes of music and the fluidity of the constructions makes a great form of analogies to musical formations.

I firstly became very interested in the linked sequence of poems, 'Day Light Songs', 'Fire Lizard' and 'A Night Square'. These poems have a huge immediate appeal thanks to their visual impact. There is light on the page. A huge sense of space is created by the opening out of the words and phrases. I feel that it was this space that made them approachable to my untrained eye. This does not look like prose so I did not read in that way. It did not even look like a poem so I did not read in that way. Although there is much more to this poetry than riding along a torrent of beautiful and stimulating rushes that is the aspect of these poems which drew me in to discover the deeper and longer lasting stimulation. I was not trying to decipher the poem; I was not trying to explain away its mysteries. Reading a poem is not like solving an elaborate cryptic crossword clue. This is true also of music. Although interpretation of music and poetry is often presented as such there is no singular answer lurking within the text to be had if the reader were only learned enough.

Physical space is opened a kind of 'temporal' space is also created. These are poems which exist in their own contexts and which run in their own tempi. Because they relate to a context created *in the poem* and not to an external context they have a rolling, musical progression. As I read these poems I find I am propelled by a particular momentum which sweeps me through to the conclusion. As the text of the poem accumulates, confidently guiding me through its particular rhythms with an almost muscular control, it is only possible to glance backwards. It is impossible to stop, to stand still, while reading these poems. It seems to me as if the poems are only visible through this rear-view window. This is a strange and beguiling experience which can only ever exist through the multiple perspectives of a shifting memory. It is a very exciting rush as the constantly shifting meanings of a poem speed in such a way as they always seem just within grasp, before disappearing as the next point of emerges, like smoke. As clouds form and reform they are in a constant process. Just as they seem to have formed a shape it immediately collapses into some new form. And just as we can catalogue cloud forms based on imaginary ideals of characteristic shapes so with language here. I suspect that no amount of analytical, pathological, forensic type investigation can really explain away the mysteries of these poems. As each word and phrase is added to my experience of the poem it relates in multifaceted ways to the words and phrases that have come before creating an extremely mobile procession of connotations. And through these interactions the poem has a beauty and interest which lies outside the normal realm of literalism. The poems push to the limit the amount of information my brain can hold on to: and so I can't hold on. This is similar to what the composers I am interested in do with music. Your choice is to either embrace this or remain in a paralysis of 'the fear of misunderstanding.'

The aspects of Prynne's poems which most often make direct influence on specific musical pieces are those aspects of patterning, formation and the construction within the whole poem. The architecture of the poems presents an analogy with a possible architecture in music. There is normally a distinction made in music between the surface texture of a piece and those underlying structural currents which may operate at a deeper and less instantly obvious level. This is a distinction which can be applied to these poems.

In *Fire Lizard*, my work for string quartet and baritone voice, I was interested in unraveling several structural layers in Prynne's poem and translating those into layers of my musical piece that would operate in an similar way. In music a structural rhythm is the rhythmic pattern created by large sections of musical time, as opposed to the actual rhythms which form part of melodies and movements and make their patterns over brief moments. The energy of a piece of music often lies in the interaction of these various layers of structural rhythm. The form of a piece is articulated over time, after all, not on stasis. On some crude level the first and closest level is the notes and rhythms, the words & small groups of words. The medium level is the melodies and the phrases, those words bound by sense or a consistency of voice perhaps, & the grand structures, the large scale relationships and the resonances which form only over the whole sweep.

In *Fire Lizard* I became interested in separating two strands of development which would eventually coexist in one musical work. One was the visual strand, the regular blocks of widely spaced text on the page. The other was an irregular 'semantic' division of the text. Here within the fleeting text I found smaller sections, phrases. This division on my part was entirely subjective and created a rather fluid sequence of phrases which vary in length in contrast regular divisions of the visual strand. The flow of words that makes up the poem is divided in two ways. The same words are interpreted twice and the interaction of the two rhythms created a further layer, a rhythm of interaction and a really deep level of counterpoint. In order to make these rhythmic layers manifest I found various types of music which I could switch between. The different characters of these types of music would then be clearly defined so that a change from one to another would make a clear 'point' in the musical timeline. These changes of music-type, of style and character, correspond to the points in the text where I found semantic change. To articulate the regular rhythmic structure I found a static element: a long held chord in the strings. This was then to interject at the points where the stanzas break on the page. As this happens irrespective of the organic, fluid development of the music the effect of these is rather mechanical, a strange and phlegmatic presence. So the first of these, "Come and tell me the draw of the beetle making the lane of water the fire lizard," is set using the first context, a highly rhythmicized type of music. The next part is, "I hear the front of your/ visited wish, I am/ inside it now.// I hear where you go to . . ." is set using the second context, an eerie and disjointed texture featuring the unnerving snapping of wood noises, since the text is bound together. They are linked together by a certain consistency of voice which goes over the edges of the printed stanzas. This phrase is therefore interrupted by the first of the long chords, the mechanical part coinciding with the breaks in stanza. This process continues with a third context, a virtuosic and lyrical module. And so the text moves through these contexts changing from one to another as the surface texture of the poem changes. The created piece embodies that almost tidal drive as material unfolds. It becomes a muscular contraction of ideas and material which creates an energetic release through its conjunction with a mechanical process. In this way the inspiration comes not in the form of specific images but in a wish to emulate somehow the energetic form of the poem.

All composers who are interested in using the human voice will turn to the topic of opera. Although some composers have shunned opera as an old-fashioned and conservative genre a few have taken great strides in recent years, fusing a modernist aesthetic with a heightened manifestation of singing on stage. After *Fire Lizard* and various other small scale works I was keen to write an opera and had been searching for a topic for an opera for some while. It was only really rather late into the process that the idea struck me to use a Prynne poem. In this large project, however, the poem became the epicenter of an explosion of projections. When it comes to opera the relationship between text and music becomes extremely conjoined. There is an expectation with an opera, and I was very interested in writing a piece which would use that particular term, in characters which develop and in plots and narratives. But what I had learned from reading these poems is that there need not only be one singular narrative in a coherent work. In Prynne's poems many voices interweave. The voices may be ones we recognize, such as those form particular disciplines (advertising slogans, technical jargon) or they be created ones given their particular character through a certain consistency in tone or a particular type of construction. The voices may not communicate with each other but they will spark coincidences and, most importantly, strange rhythmic relationships will emerge. In my opera, *A Night Square,* became a source-book. Text around which I used various other sources to create six strands that could interweave like the voices in Prynne's poem. When I was writing the piece, before it was complete, the question I was most frequently asked was, "what is it about?" I resented this question at first. I thought it was inappropriate and missed the point. After all, my opera had no story, no themes, no narrative. It is *about* nothing and *about* everything, I would respond, unhelpfully. But I have come to see that it was, in fact, an appropriate question that comes close to an important realization. The crucial thing of the poems is what they are *about.* That is to say, yes, what they are, but, at the same time what they surround and what they nearly are. The subject they come close too is at once more important and more ambiguous.

This is true of *Chromatin,* the poem that has most recently influenced a piece of mine. The range of this poem is remarkable. From the smallest structure of the human body, the unfolding cell divisions of the nucleus, it takes us grandly to vast metaphysical structures: 'the Homeric ice-field'. *Chromatin* does not look so unusual as the former poems. It sits quite squarely in a little block of text on a single page.

The language is at once terse and expansive: claustrophobic at the start becoming, through a nuclear unfolding of energy, expansive and lyrical. Themes in the poem resonate with many of my musical concerns. The changes of scale as we view objects from multiple perspectives. Also, the processes by which learning can take place and the complimentary process by which patterns disintegrate. The degradation of pattern has a clear musical analogy as musical themes develop and their authenticity is challenged by increasingly aggressive variety. The 'quick-cutting' between the mystical sterility of the 'prism crystal' and the hysterical outbursts of 'mental confusion' present an instant possibility of snapping between musical contexts: a musical drama. What makes this poem somewhat different, though, was that it inspired me to do all these things but maintain a consistency of 'the whole.' So while as in *Fire Lizard* and *Night Square* I translate the multiple voices into multiple musics here they are working more towards a poetic whole. The parts within this poem are all contributing, in their fragmentary way, to a broad sweep of poetic energy. As usual it was the mechanisms by which the poem worked that found themselves becoming analogies for musical schemes. *Chromatin* is my most developed interaction between a Prynne poem and a specific work and the two are so tied up. What I wanted to create was a parallel version of the same text through music. This would in the totality of the musical exposition retain the arc of the poem and although using the words to create a vocal line the musical substance itself would surpass the specific words.

These are specific works of mine where Prynne's text has formed a core. But it is difficult to fully explain the reasons why a composer would need to interact so much with a poet. The poet after all is writing in a completely different medium. But with music and poetry the media are complimentary and can become symbiotic. Individual poems can serve as models for challenging new schemata. The schemes may then spur invention into new fields that would not have been possible without the initial stimulus. In parallel an interaction with a poet's aesthetic and a familiarity with the poet's toolbox will help at every point to make those difficult creative decisions, just helping to steer the artist and help reduce the chance of stasis. Prynne's poems are a particularly useful source of inspiration because they manifest themselves in such multifaceted ways. Because there is no easily attainable definitive reading the poems are always fresh and alive. There is such a wealth of stimulation amongst the many faces and the stimulation of unendingly various types.

Aside form technical developments that have come from such a vivid tapestry there I have found a further inspiration. That works like these could be created takes a bravery that can only be accounted for by a singular visionary. Seeking constantly to renew his critical apparatus is a challenge for any artist. It is so reassuring, therefore, to see such versatility in the works J.H. Prynne. There is an unerring commitment to invention. He has not succumbed to forces of conservatism or banality. As those forces of ordinariness and self-obsession strengthen unrelentingly the work of J.H. Prynne can stand firm. In Prynne's work I found a wonderfully profound exploration of the process of invention. The poems are aspirational. The constant requirement for exploration is never lost in these poems and as they take widely divergent paths around a massive network of topics and schemes they hold, in their entirety, to a course of beautiful lyrical intelligence.

COMPOSING WITH PRYNNE

Erik Ulman

> The arts aspire, if not to complement one another,
> at least to lend one another new energies. —Baudelaire[1]

Writing of Wyndham Lewis' drawings after *Timon of Athens*, Hugh Kenner described the play's function for Lewis as a "paradigm of coherence to steady his judgment and fletch his will."[2] As a composer I often employ similar "paradigms of coherence." Composition is typically an extremely mediated activity, passing through both manuscript and the minds, bodies, and instruments of others before manifestation; and for energy not to be lost but intensified through such indirection is a difficult and precarious undertaking. Other artworks can, at least for me, serve as both model and fuel through this labyrinth of intangibility and deferment.

J.H. Prynne's poetry is one of my favorite sources of inspiration. Four of my pieces are rooted specifically in his poems: *L'Extase de M. Poher* (originally written in 2002 and completely re-composed in 2006) and its variant and sequel *Deuxième Extase* (2003), both for solo cello; *Thoughts on the Esterházy Court Uniform* (2004) for clarinet/ bass clarinet, electric guitar, piano, violin, and cello; and a brief setting of *Smooth Landing* (2004) for soprano, piano, violin, and cello. Several future projects are also tied to Prynne's work: a set of small piano pieces; chamber orchestral works named for *Red D Gypsum* and *Unanswering Rational Shore*; and a *Troisième Extase* for cello and seven cellos on tape, further building (or feeding) on its predecessors. Some relationships between text and music are casual, even arbitrary; others approach programmatic absorption of a poem's themes and energy.

Prynne's work is notable for its often bewildering density and vigor. He has stated, "It has mostly been my own aspiration, for example, to establish relations not personally with the reader, but with the world and its layers of shifted but recognisable usage; and thereby with the reader's own position within this world."[3] This project results in poems that both depict and enact the constant mutual interference of radically different forces, from geological process to neurology, from the market to literary history, from anecdotal experience to abstraction.

I haven't yet matched this richness in my own work, but it remains an inspiration and hope. Language, Prynne writes, "is a pluralised system, invested with contradictions which are themselves the diagram of its energetic over-determination."[4] If music's inadequacy as a representational medium dooms any aspiration to literal equivalence, a sufficiently "energetic over-determination" of compositional means, looking to Prynne for one "paradigm of coherence," may still achieve comparable abundance. An incidental benefit is that composing "after Prynne" contributes to my understanding of his poems, since it involves a transcription, albeit a not wholly articulate one, of features and relationships. As such it externalizes William Empson's principle that "the process of getting to understand a poet is precisely that of constructing his poems in one's own mind."[5]

Prynne's work serves me particularly well for my music not least because of strong analogies between reading Prynne and composing a piece. Both demand numerous engagements of different speed and focus, both fleeting insight and patient labor. My first reading of a Prynne poem is fast, identifying general features of diction, registering its bracing rhythmic energy. I am likely to be extremely deficient in many of its constituent disciplines; however, I can immediately recognize the humor and anger of their juxtapositions. Heartened by this direct impact, I begin a second reading testing for relevant connotations, holding in mind diverging implications from a single node, making conjectures of concealed intention from the eddies and resistances of minute surface contradiction or emphasis.[6] If several words, however scattered through a sequence, belong to the same family of associations, they describe a thematic strand whose significance, affect, and interactions with others remain to be determined. For a third reading it is usually time to get out the dictionary, checking the words I don't know as well as the etymologies and secondary or archaic meanings of those I do. Gradually a sense of the poem accumulates. Understanding remains partial and contingent, and no angle of view can account for every detail; but this simply means that the writing remains vibrant, always responsive to new ventures and productive of new knowledge. As I live with them, passages that had once seemed impossible to penetrate begin to yield, or else to make clear the purpose of their intransigence.

My compositional process likewise presupposes numerous passes requiring various kinds of involvement, and comes less to perfect stability than to what Jean Barraqué once called "incessant incompletion."[7] Work for me is usually an extremely layered and indirect process, building from local decisions toward imagined wholes, which mutate and collapse as I fill them out.

I often compose my first drafts very rapidly, much as I first read Prynne. I may improvise material on the page within such metric schemes as I will describe later, or sketch general shapes suggested, perhaps, by a Prynne poem, or even by a word—"dots," for example, might elicit, unimaginatively enough, disconnected points of sound. Sometimes I improvise on existing musical fragments—bars from my earlier work, say, or a row or fragment from Schoenberg. These references multiply my criteria for decisions: my associations may guide and inspire me, and something of the original, like patterns fragmented in a Cubist collage, will carry into the final design.

Such trivial beginnings provide initial definitions of material for subsequent elaboration. I now revise my fragments in light of one another, shuffling them, grouping them into continuities, filling in gaps, inventing beginnings or endings for them. As these bits coalesce into larger musical objects, they accrete meaning not present in their initial formulation, which I adjust both through close, intuitive working and through automatic procedures akin to William Burroughs' "fold-in" method:

> For example I take page one and fold it into page one hundred—I insert the resulting composite as page ten— When the reader reads page ten he is flashing forward in time to page one hundred and back in time to page one—the déjà vu phenomenon can so be produced to order—This method is of course used in music, where we are continually moved backward and forward on the time track by repetition and rearrangements of musical themes—[8]

For Burroughs, random variation, an almost autonomous textual self-production, subsumes the traditionally architectural and rhetorical functions of recollection and emphasis. My fragmentation and redistribution of material also allows for variations of meaning to arise "on their own"; but, as with Burroughs, it is not a question of merely accepting the results, but of weighing and integrating them. Recurrences may function as neutral coherence, or else may intensify into a specific recollection. I reread my drafts, trying to feel their trajectories and resonances; and as pitch and color achieve definition, rhythms and form may need revision. This may be subtle (the addition or subtraction of a beat) or drastic (the re-shuffling of large sections, or the introduction of new ones, or the complete omission of others). As I read I write, adding hypothetical tempi and dynamics as well as wholly new material that can enrich or focus what I have made; and, as with reading Prynne, these hypotheses are either confirmed by corroborative details or discarded as irrelevant. Secondary levels may assume more character than the initial draft, demanding that I radically alter notes and rhythms to make from them the gestures they implied but do not equal. Since each note may participate in numerous trajectories, a small revision can have enormous consequences, posing for me problems of interpretation much like those that confront a sensitive and sympathetic performer, who must recognize and project as many lines of force as possible.

This description is oversimplified; the point is that shifts of focus between rough intuitions and minute detail-work are common to both my reading of Prynne and my composing, as is a sense of the task as an open-ended, empirical process of discovery.

If reading Prynne and composing resemble one another, structural and thematic features of his poems are also relevant to my composition. One is the recontextualization of dismantled material. I don't know to what extent Prynne may use chance procedures; but throughout his work one can find embedded fragments of other writing. One example is the passage from *All's Well that Ends Well* which undergirds the longest section of *The Oval Window*.[9] Another comes from Steve Reich's tape piece *Come Out* (1966), in which recorded speech is played against itself, creating ever new alignments as it goes out of phase. Reich's source is the words of a young black man injured by police in a Harlem riot. Only those who were visibly bleeding were taken to the hospital; so, he explains, "I had to, like, open the bruise up and let some of the bruise blood come out to show them."[10] Compare these circumstances and this exact statement with a passage from the seventh stanza of *For the Monogram* (which, indeed, features the words "come out" in its first line):

> peel back this vivid failed bruise, baleful
> to scale and burning. You got scarlet out to show it
> in the toy-pack acerbic notation, in less significant to
> hands off warning come out for out now long and easy
> bleed pastime, henceforth to show round a bone stricture
> flaunted out and peeled easily off from these shores.[11]

Two stanzas later we read:

> Cheeks plunder a sealed throat
> gape losing tone at multiple asters out to show willing
> and process each destruction; sorrow blunts link
> maps as pressed candles require a first fire come right
> out to show to climb down in space trial bondage.[12]

The reference reveals a new layer of meaning, corroborating other images of violence, as well as a loose but suggestive parallel between the obsessive repetitions in Reich's style and the more submerged but still striking recurrences in Prynne's. In any case, it is as though Prynne has digested Reich's material, and around its fragments has gathered new contexts, extensions, and complications.

Both Prynne and I have an interest in discarded, impure material, remainders of other intentions, whose original implications remain partially legible. Recycling and, more generally, the stratified and discontinuous working method of which it is an instance indicate productive and destructive tensions in work and world. In "L'Extase de M. Poher" we read:

> No
> poetic gabble will survive which fails
> to collide head-on with the unwitty circus . . .[13]

Reeve and Kerridge paraphrase: "In order to survive, poetry has to
'collide' with the powerful instrumental discourses of the culture
(smashing them into pieces), rather than dodging into alley-ways
while they pass, or lingering in safe places like gardens."[14] This collision
produces rubbish, whose value in the poem shifts from negative to
positive:

Rubbish is

pertinent; essential; the

most intricate presence in

our entire culture; the

ultimate sexual point of the whole place turned

into a model question.[15]

Rubbish provokes complex and intimate congress among hitherto
separate discourses and levels of experience: against the passivity
implicit earlier in the poem ("No / question provokes the alpha
rhythm . . ."),[16] rubbish becomes a site of engagement, "undiluted and
intoxicating," an image of "a society in which such unlikely integrity
could have a use."[17]

I wrote the first version of my cello piece *L'Extase de M. Poher*
for Charles Curtis in 2001–2, and in 2006 rewrote it so thoroughly
that little resemblance to the original remains; Séverine Ballon gave its
premiere, magnificently, in Clermont-Ferrand in 2007. I compressed
some diffuse passages while opening larger stases as compensation,
and tied my work's unfolding more strictly to the poem's structure. If
extending the social implications of Prynne's rubbish remains beyond
my means, except in vague and metaphorical ways, the protracted
and rather violent compositional process nonetheless yields a musical
"smash-up" true to a sequence of commands in the poem: "Crush
tread trample distinguish." My sequels to *L'Extase* propose further
exploration of such tensions—distinctions as violence, destruction
as perception. While the *Deuxième Extase* (premiered in 2004 by
Frank Cox) tends to isolate the pacific moments of its now discarded
predecessor, the third, with its overlayering of pre-recorded cellos, will
take compaction to an extreme, forcing together fragments from the
whole disjunct compositional span, less a tidy reconciliation ("we are
too kissed & fondled") than a head-on collision.

Example: *L'Extase de M. Poher*, mm. 242–270

I have learned much not only from Prynne's interest in rubbish, but also from the sound of his verse, which ranges from the gentle *Day Light Songs* to the aggressive irregularities of more recent sequences. Such blanket characterizations, however, obscure dissonances essential throughout Prynne's output. The delicacy of the *Day Light Songs*, for instance, must withstand and articulate itself through resistances—broken words, unexpected diction ("polythene")—that threaten balances in sound and sense.[18] Conversely, the sharp consonants, wrenching enjambements, and heavy trochees of *Red D Gypsum* may open unexpectedly into mellifluity, as with the cunning vowel leading of "flawless glucose shimmered sky" in the last line of the first stanza.[19] Prynne is capable of a lyricism rare among contemporary poets, but always tests it against more abrupt energies.

I also balance lyrical and disruptive impulses in my attempt at a "very close music."[20] My first steps are usually rhythmic; and I often derive my metric scheme from the length of words in a text, in which one letter is equivalent to one sixteenth-note unit. "I walk on up," for example, would yield four bars in the sequence 1/16, 2/8, 1/8, and 1/8. This practice has several congenial features. It produces, at

151

Example: Erik Ulman, *Smooth Landing*, mm. 1–15

the very least, a fundamental, energizing irregularity; it also tends to
privilege shorter meters, which focuses my rhythmic detail. Starting
with meter, rather than with motives or larger formal units, gives me
a flexible middle ground from which I can address both.

Smooth Landing may furnish an example. I wanted to make
something for Prynne after visiting him in Cambridge in Summer
2004, and used "Smooth Landing" to make a song.[21] I chose it not
least because it suited my formal needs: it was compact, and its formal
regularity (four stanzas of four lines each) and openness on the page
(its lines are double spaced) seemed well-suited for the textural
transparency I had already imagined for the music. I derived all the
rhythms from the text. As described above, meters equalled the lengths
of words (with one added bar and a few conflations of adjacent bars
into longer units); each bar was divided into a pulse equal to the
numerator either of that bar or the one preceding or following; and
then I picked out individual points from that structure by scanning it
with the same numerators.

In this way, arbitrary conditions come to accrete significance, as I fold their terms back into new levels of structure; and their initial arbitrariness guarantees for my musical invention a certain healthy independence from the text. After all, the point of my modelling is, to borrow from Tom Raworth, "not to recall / but to trigger."[22]

In *Smooth Landing* I left my rhythmic scheme much closer to the audible surface than was previously usual for me, allowing as elaborations only a few accelerations and decelerations. The result is a very dry, non-lyrical texture, although near the end melismas become increasingly available. The cello was added midway through the compositional process. I felt the need for something outside the basic structures I had set up, something occasionally integrated into them (either rhythmically or through some kind of complementarity of pitch), but more often standing apart, as a foreign vantage—as glissandi, or clouds of grace notes, or, at the end, as a bass drone which eventually sprouts, for the first time, microtonal distortions. The pitch material is basically the row from Schoenberg's *Moses und Aron*, a piece I have long admired and had discussed in Cambridge with Prynne, and which material I have used many times before. The text setting is not conventionally gracious: once I had derived my basic structure, I composed without specific reference to the text, wanting more flexible relations between words and music than might happen otherwise. However, a few cues do get obliquely illustrated. The opening line's "lie of the immortal," for example, provoked both some repetitions in violin and piano and a sustained slide in the cello—although perhaps one or the other is the corresponding truth?

If Prynne's poetry is rich in musical features, it also resembles music in its simultaneous urgency and indeterminacy of address. Prynne rarely if ever expunges meaning and syntax as totally as did Stein, Cage, or Mac Low; and he has been a sharp critic of much of the Language poetry that has followed in the wake of such experiment. Against its narrow reflexivity and pretensions to a "general economy of de-signification," Prynne writes that

> external reference is one of [language's] stabilising axes, just as are also the internal enrichments of indeterminacy, and of self-reference. And within the domains of partial or even

very substantial indeterminacy the textures and formalisms
of multiplicity rather seldom cancel by exact reciprocation;
more often there are tendencies to culminate and synergise,
percolating by reticular connections and antagonisms across
the channels of prescribed signification so as to challenge and
displace the whole fabric of interpretation but not at all to
extirpate it.[23]

Instead, Prynne approaches music's indefinite power through overload,
so that the speed and ambiguity of collisions, although inviting
sustained study and interpretation, elicit emotions, thought, and
analogical perception before they resolve (if ever) into an unambiguous
meaning. I am reminded of a passage from Theodor Adorno's essay
on Alban Berg's compositional technique: "Total continuity, the most
concentrated rigour in the progression of the music, that is to say,
organization to an extreme degree, and all this is not just combined
with a jungle-like density, a tendency towards the chaotic—the two
are actually equated."[24]

One of Prynne's methods is extreme syntactical compression. In
Blue Slides at Rest, for example, he collapses a phrase: "day butters a
slice."[25] What Empson writes of meter in traditional verse may be
relevant to Prynne's distortions of "normal colloquial English": "the
reader thinks of the various colloquial forms which are near to it,
and puts them together, weighting their probabilities in proportion
to their nearness."[26] Prynne's light punctuation also intensifies this
compaction. Although sometimes punctuation reinforces the punning
multiplicity of his language ("Egged on to say no, cream on top"),[27]
often Prynne installs his words in less determinate constellations—
does one read a word as verb or noun or both, and in what layers of
significance is it active? In the preface to *Bending the Bow*, Robert
Duncan writes:

> The immediate event—the phrase within its line, the adjoining
> pulse in silence, the new phrase—each part is a thing in
> itself; the junctures not binding but freeing the elements of
> configuration so that they participate in more than one figure
> ... [The poet] strives not for a disintegration of syntax but for

a complication within syntax, overlapping structures, so that words are freed, having bounds out of bound.[28]

Something similar might be said of Prynne, but in his case "freeing" and "binding" are equally in evidence. Duncan's frequently loose distribution of events on a page is contrary to Prynne's increasing reliance on standardized stanzaic lengths, whose density and regularity no less keep the energies of his constellations taut and coiled than does a language high-keyed both in sound and in its aggressive tone of emergency and advertisement. Urgent but indeterminate exhortations assault us: "Make a dot / difference, make an offer";[29] or "Lay down."[30] Solecism? or, if not, lay down what? Further, archaic meanings as well as a full range of specialist vocabularies screen meaning from immediate absorption. Sometimes Prynne's choices alienate the familiar: in *Blue Slides at Rest*, we read not of milk but of "Reaching colloid to serve."[31] Elsewhere, professional terminology likely strikes the reader first as a generalized representative of a given discourse (here apparently both medicine and insurance) and as an intransigent music:

> OK the recipient must guarantee, to be bound
> by reciprocal hand contracture head to head G21
> lodging 5HT single note purification alongside
> microfibril, merge botanics.[32]

In context Prynne's variety of diction is another instance of positive rubbish, manifesting both dissonance and fusion within its heterogeneity, both common and conflicting lines of force, rhymes.

All this may in various ways inspire me; but I would like to come back to specific parallels between Prynne's forms or themes and my own. In my *Red D Gypsum* in progress, I have begun with a structural grid of thirty equally sized sections, containing musical events suggested by images or recurrences in the poems. Prynne's sequence is shot through with both strictly focused and more open-ended resemblances and repetitions, nodes around which the rest functions. Examples would include the passage from "flawless" to "broken sky" in the first and last stanzas,[33] as well as numerous appearances of the letter D and variants of "re" (itself a term for the note D) and "red."[34] These imply thematic reservoirs beneath the poem's surface, and create a variety of echoes and prefigurations. In my versions, transcriptions of these impressions may shift or disappear, but should leave resonant traces. Once again, I am not aiming at illustration; nor do I feel constrained to stick to the original's uniform stanza length. In Prynne, such apparent uniformity demands multiple speeds of reading; but music must, as it were, do its reading itself, building variation of successive and simultaneous tempo into its own fabric.

Besides offering formal models, Prynne's themes have also been immensely suggestive to me as a composer. I have mentioned the significance of rubbish; but another central preoccupation in Prynne's poetry is the tension between knowledge and unmediated experience. In "L'Extase de M. Poher" we read:

> the immediate body of wealth is not
> history, body-fluid not dynastic.[35]

This asserts that value lies not in official order but in physicality itself, evoking Olson's sense of the body in "Projective Verse" or "Proprioception."[36] But the non-conceptual freshness of "body-fluid" must coexist with social and historical fact, not least as manifested in language and the "accumulated potential signification stored in the history of [words'] past usage."[37] Prynne accommodates both, without glossing over their conflicts. Interjections offer poetic precedent. "[The] use of lyrical *O*," he writes, "[is] a marker for the boundary of one discourse where it is momentarily exceeded by another,"[38] suggestive both of "prelinguistic expressivity . . . as if directly connected to the involuntary reflexes" and of elevation "towards sublimity, for laying claim to the power of a primal *planctus*."[39] It is

> a form of acknowledgment and dialectical holding to the locus
> of a demanding but possible truth, at least as much as simply
> the expression of some feeling about a moment particularly
> stressed by the pressures of experience . . . This kind of
> interjection can carry multiple stress, at high or low pitch,
> because convention has kept it separated from grammatical
> linkages which would cant its force sideways and absorb it
> into the coded frameworks of sentence structure.[40]

These complex, liminal moments that escape "grammatical linkages" beyond and under language's normal articulateness bring music to mind; and music, like emphatical language, is a site in which syntax and the radiant, expressively self-contained phenomenon intersect, to their mutual enrichment and frustration.[41] In his "Thoughts on the Esterházy Court Uniform," Prynne casts this tension in terms of music as both "home" and a "complete migration of sound," containing both recall's substitution for experience and the immortality intimated by rhyme, the stability of "a decent and proper order" and the freedom of unmediated experience.[42] Such negotiations are for Prynne both subject and method: his poem is a dense thicket of almost graspable imprecision, constantly inviting and eluding logical unravelling—its texture is its meaning, a sluggish energy, at once home and migration. As Reeve and Kerridge write,

> The techniques of the writing—the indeterminable referents of deictic terms like 'it' and 'there', and the characteristic ways in which the turns of the line-ends enact the constant slippage of what looked secure, underpin the engagement with a problematically intermediate position between stasis and flow.[43]

My quintet *Thoughts on the Esterházy Court Uniform*, written in 2003-4 for Ensemble Plus-Minus, may be among my works the piece that draws deepest motivation from Prynne. The title alludes to Haydn, court composer to the Esterházys; and in consequence I derived some of my piece, ultimately pretty unrecognizably, from a descending figure in the second movement of his String Quartet, Op. 74 #3 (bars 9 and 10), which embodies for me a special "grace & hesitation" of descent. Further, the end of Haydn's *Farewell* Symphony suggested that of my piece. Prynne describes the former with his lines

all put out their lights
and take their instruments away with them,

while his title alludes to the servitude that prompted this extraordinary music:

157

> [Nicholas Esterházy] would frequently retire to [his] palace, dragging along with him his retinue and all his musicians. Haydn and the others, having left their families behind, often wished to return home and on one occasion, to encourage his patron to leave the Esterház retreat, he composed his *Farewell Symphony* (No. 45), in which the desires of the musicians were cleverly conveyed by having the instruments drop out of the final movement one by one until only a few strings remained.[44]

I may not be able to match Haydn's inventive and humane elegance; but, in tribute, my ensemble also dwindles, leaving the piano mostly alone in the work's final pages, although violin and cello join it in the closing bars.

The piece went, as usual, through numerous labyrinthine drafts and revisions that I intercut and overlaid. Ultimately, I found it useful to identify fourteen key moments in the text which suggested, dimly or clearly, musical analogies, and aligned or invented material to correspond to them. Implicit in Prynne's earlier writings, however, as in Olson's projective verse, is the sense of the work finding its own form. I wanted the piece to embody energies analogous to those in the poem, fusing creation and exegesis; but if these energies took me away from fidelity to the model, I let them. The poem's governing idea of "return" led me to structure the piece as a kind of rondo, with literal recurrences either of material or of generative procedure. "Complete migration," in turn, suggested the overwiping of those recurrent elements by either revision or a deliberately disorientating and undifferentiated surface:

> if it would only
> level out into some complete migration of
> sound. I could then leave unnoticed, bring nothing
> with me, allow the world free of its displace-
> ment.[45]

In the music that corresponds to this passage, the sustaining instruments play glissandi at maximum volume, obliterating distinctions in their "complete migration," while the piano offers decontextualized distortions of material from elsewhere in the piece—an admission, perhaps, that recollection and anticipation always taint "complete migration." This, however, may be not only necessary but beneficent as well: "home," however deadening its "decent and proper / order," can establish itself "in some quite / specific place," enabling us "not to carry it / everywhere with us." Only then may we have the unencumbered experience we have desired, without renouncing the meaning arising through recurrence:

> maybe we can listen to the rain
> without always thinking about rain, we
> trifle with rhyme and again is the
> sound of immortality.[46]

Prynne's poetry seems to me exemplary, of a rare fullness and invention. My initial encounters with it have often baffled me, and there are many sequences into which I have as yet only rudimentary insight; but my imperfect understanding mutes neither his work's immediate nor more gradual power. Few poets use language—as sound, as social fact, as historical object, as representation, as manifestation—with such thoroughness and agility. Prynne's works invite and endure exacting attention, in Empson's words, "with undiminished reputation.[47] If much Language poetry takes modernist achievement into a realm of diminishing returns—the complacent impenetrability of a mere "free play" of surfaces, or the repetitive exposure of the emptiness of social tropes, the poetic "mainstream" in England and America is striking for the vacuity of its rhetoric and technique. Prynne avoids both culs-de-sac. His letter to Steve McCaffery is perhaps the keenest critique yet made of the former's aspirations to "the *open* text, the *inventive*, *selective* reader," as he disputes "the quality and competence of the freedom claimed to be thus established";[48] and where the latter coasts on precedent without renewing its perceptions and vitality, Prynne's deep engagement with both English and foreign tradition succumbs neither to enervated nostalgia nor sterile academicism, but forges of both experiment and heritage a coherent, moving, and provocative practice. As a composer I continue to learn from his example, and to delight in, and envy, his achievement.

Notes

1 Quoted in H.H. Arnason, *Robert Motherwell* (New York: Harry N. Abrams, 1977), p.96.
2 Hugh Kenner, 'The Visual World of Wyndham Lewis', in Walter Michel, *Wyndham Lewis: Paintings and Drawings* (Berkeley: University of California, 1971), p.23.
3 Quoted at Nate Dorward's invaluable website, 'J.H. Prynne: A Checklist', http://www.ndorward.com/poetry/articles_etc/prynne_checklist.htm (accessed August 23, 2005).
4 J.H. Prynne, 'Letter to Steve McCaffery', in *The Gig* #7, November 2000, p.44.
5 William Empson, *Seven Types of Ambiguity* (New York: New Directions, n.d. [original edition: 1930]), p.62.
6 Prynne's study of Shakespeare's 94th Sonnet is an object lesson in the teasing out and articulation of such implications, and as such illuminates not only Shakespeare but Prynne as well. See *They That Haue Powre to Hurt* (Cambridge, 2001).
7 Quoted in Paul Griffiths, *Modern Music and After* (Oxford: Oxford University Press, 1995), p.230.
8 William S. Burroughs, 'The Future of the Novel', in *Word Virus* (New York: Grove, 1998), p.272.
9 See N.H. Reeve and Richard Kerridge's analysis in *Nearly Too Much: The Poetry of J.H. Prynne* (Liverpool: Liverpool University Press, 1995), pp.162–3.
10 The work is described, though with a slightly inaccurate source text, in Glenn Watkins, *Soundings: Music in the Twentieth Century* (New York: Schirmer, 1988), pp.600–1; it is available in *Steve Reich 1965–1995* (Nonesuch CD 79451).
11 J.H. Prynne, *Poems* (Tarset: Bloodaxe Books, 2005), p.424.
12 *Poems*, p.426.
13 Ibid., p.162.
14 Reeve and Kerridge, p.9.
15 *Poems*, p.162.
16 Ibid., p.161.
17 These quotations are from Out to Lunch, 'Garbage: A Discussion of Value', address to the Birkbeck Centre for Contemporary Poetics Research, November 1, 2000, http://www.pores.bbk.ac.uk/1/index.html (accessed August 21, 2005).
18 *Poems*, p.27.
19 Ibid., p.435.
20 To cite Charles Olson on late Shakespeare. In *Henry VIII*, Olson finds an

aural vigor and richness that are no less characteristic of Prynne: "[The words] 'by violent' (which is only 1 accent and 4 syllables) already shows forth the weave of accent, quantity, breath which makes prosody the music it is: and here is a very close music, sharp, long and stopped, all in a small space of time, reflecting the truth it is, that this art, when it is at its best, is powerful just because it does obey space-time." In 'Quantity in Verse, and Shakespeare's Late Plays', in *Collected Prose*, eds. Donald M. Allen and Benjamin Friedlander (Berkeley: University of California Press, 1997), p. 274.

[21] *Poems*, p.191.

[22] Tom Raworth, "Homily," in *Collected Poems* (Manchester: Carcanet, 2003), p.104.

[23] "Letter," p.44.

[24] Theodor W. Adorno, "Berg's Discoveries in Compositional Technique," in *Quasi una fantasia: Essays on Modern Music,* tr. Rodney Livingstone (London: Verso, 1992), p.184.

[25] *Poems*, p.568.

[26] Empson, p.28.

[27] Poems, p.563.

[28] Robert Duncan, *Bending the Bow* (New York: New Directions, 1968), p.ix.

[29] *Poems*, p.519.

[30] Ibid., p.446.

[31] Ibid., p.568.

[32] Ibid., p.559.

[33] Ibid., pp.435, 449.

[34] See Jay Basu, "The Red Shift: Trekking J.H. Prynne's *Red D Gypsum*," in *The Cambridge Quarterly*, Vol. 30, No. 1, 2001, pp.19–36.

[35] *Poems*, p.162.

[36] See Olson, especially pp.240–2 and 181–3.

[37] J.H. Prynne, *Stars, Tigers and the Shape of Words* (London: Birkbeck College, 1993), p.16.

[38] J.H. Prynne, "English Poetry and Emphatical Language," in *Proceedings of the British Academy*, LXXIV, 1988, p.168.

[39] Ibid., p.166.

[40] Ibid., pp.167–8.

[41] A suggestive treatment of this tension can be found in Adorno's 'Music and Language: A Fragment'. Adorno identifies in music's "direct expression" a theological dimension, an aspiration to be "a language without intention." However, the very immediacy that invokes this dimension is powerless to realize it fully: without developing a complex "system of interconnections," music would deteriorate from its glimpse of the

absolute into a "mere succession of sensuous stimuli," an acoustic kaleidoscope. While language from its outset "mediates the absolute," music "finds the absolute immediately, but at the moment of discovery it becomes obscured"; but for Adorno it is this enmeshing of radiant phenomenon in a mediating syntax that enables music to unfold its essential implications, which are not only aesthetic and theological but social. Adorno, pp.1–6.

[42] See *Poems*, pp.99–100.

[43] Reeve and Kerridge, p.64.

[44] Luciano Alberti, *Music of the Western World* (New York: Crown, 1974), p.154.

[45] *Poems*, p.100.

[46] Ibid.

[47] Empson, pp.29–30.

[48] "Letter," p. 41.

CROSSWORDING. PATHS THROUGH *RED D GYPSUM*.

Nigel Wheale

1: 'underside selvage obscure' (4.5)

J.H. Prynne's first collection, *Force of Circumstance* (1962), can be read as a book of its moment, articulating English poetry's mid-century forms and preoccupations, though even this 'apprentice' book is thoroughly distinctive. The poet has chosen not to reprint *Force of Circumstance*, which suggests a kind of repudiation, despite the fact that it is full of interest. But in 1968, the year so often trumpeted as a new dawn for politics and culture throughout America and Europe, Prynne brought out three remarkable works w*f*hich were utterly distinctive, decisively breaking with established practices and expectations for English poetry, and which set the pattern for his subsequent development. These were *Kitchen Poems* (Cape Goliard, London and New York), *Day Light Songs* (Pampisford, R Books), and *Aristeas* (Ferry Press, London). *Force of Circumstance* had been published by Routledge and Kegan Paul, an established and well-respected London publisher, whereas the three innovative works appeared from a new kind of imprint, 'small' presses run by one or two enthusiasts operating outside the parameters of conventional publishing.

Despite the striking originality of Prynne's three collections from 1968, there is a view that argues for a deep continuity of content, if not form, maintained from his more conventional beginnings, and which is allied with an apparently more conservative tradition of English poetry, as represented by Philip Larkin and 'the Movement' (Clark 2003, and contra, Duncan 2003). Prynne's two following collections, *The White Stones* (1969) and *Brass* (1971), were substantial, clearly staking major claims; they consolidated Prynne's poetic, and are probably the most widely valued of his works to date.

Prynne has consistently brought out new poems, often called 'sequences' in critical discussions about them, every couple of years since then, each one presenting new kinds of challenge for the reader. *Wound Response*, including *The 'Plant Time Manifold' Transcripts* (1974), drew ever more deeply on technical discourses from biochemistry and physiology, *High Pink on Chrome* (1975) on the impact of agro-chemicals and agri-business. *The Oval Window* (1983) seemed to be work on a different scale again, and attracted one of the first really helpful monographs, by N.H. Reeve and Richard Kerridge, *Nearly Too Much, The Poetry of J.H. Prynne* (1995). This was salutary, because prior to Reeve and Kerridge's readings, *The Oval Window* had appeared to be another baffling poem. An apparently intractable text suddenly became clearer, and we must wonder how true this might be for the later poems that seem to be intransigent now. Prynne continues to challenge his readers: there is a poem in runes, another in Chinese calligraphy, pages of complex equations, all still waiting for readers and responses. In the midst of these works there are four sequences, *Day Light Songs* (1968), *Fire Lizard* (1970), *A Night Square* (1971) and *Into The Day* (1972), written with an apparent directness, and which I've always found to be intensely pleasurable in their complicated simplicity. (For a bold but demanding overview of Prynne's writing, see Nolan 2003, discussed by Wilkinson 2006).

But Prynne's collections of the last ten years have received less attention, and are often met with bemusement:

> Of course, Prynne's aesthetic of difficulty often causes panic anxiety, feels like sensory deprivation, and invites misconstruction . . . people have different perceptions of what 'good pattern' is, and may experience incompleteness as anxiety as well as cognitive freedom. I know I can't understand late Prynne, and attempts by other people to explain it seem dishonest and like fistfuls of straw. (Duncan 2003)

And so, possessing no privileged information, and setting out to read one of the recent 'late, late' works with some expectations and an open mind, I decided to opt for *Red D Gypsum*, from 1998, a collection about which I knew nothing and for which I had found hardly any discussion. I wanted to be able to read the poem, as it were, starting from nowhere (Orkney, to be precise), and only accessing the kinds of reference resources and internet provision that a decent local lending library ought to be able to offer. That's to say, you shouldn't need to have access to a major university library to undergo the occasionally strenuous thought that Prynne's poetry invites you to enjoy. Andrew Duncan comments that the work of hundreds of major 'thinkers' informs Prynne's collected *Poems* of 1998, and pursuing the reading and literatures implicit in this poetry is one of its major rewards, but that should be secondary to the experience of coming to terms with the poem in the first instance. It may that these are the perfect poems for Web junkies!

Red D Gypsum presents a sequence of thirty stanzas, each of eight lines, generally of between twelve and fourteen syllables, without end rhyming. There is no obvious conventional metrical pattern at work, though there are all kinds of subtle metrical effects. The pamphlet was first published by Keston Sutherland and Andrea Brady's *Barque* press in Cambridge, 1998, and bore as cover image a capital D 'on its matt red square' (stanza 11, line 4; quotations from the poem hereafter by stanza and line; pp.[433]–449 in *Poems* (2005)). The pamphlet (and *Poems*) print two stanzas per page, four per opening, and these have the appearance of text-blocks rather than verses, densely-marked plates of code or signs, like the wedge-impressed tablets first used when writing began in fourth millennium Mesopotamia. These verse paragraphs set a text template that is invariable, through which the poetry and our readings must run. It's a form with a rather forbidding appearance on the page, and one that characterizes some of Prynne's sequences since the 1990s, as if the writer had found an amenable convention for his demanding practice, as in *Her Weasels Wild Returning* (1994), *For the Monogram* (1997), *Triodes* (1999)—with a more variable verse line—*Unanswering Rational Shore* (2001), *Acrylic Tips* (2002), and the most recent work, *To Pollen* (2006).

It is worth thinking about the nature of the sequence in these works, in what sense the sequence may be a cumulative experience for the reader, or whether it requires a different sort of reading strategy. Poets construct all kinds of assemblage when making a 'collection' of poems. At the lowest level of motivation a book of poems simply contains the new work written during a particular period, and the shared themes and preoccupations that were specific to that time for the poet. At a more consciously organizing level, the poet might aim to write a collection focused on very specific themes, as given notice by the collection's title. This may be the case with *The White Stones* and *Brass* in particular, a title which clangs back through canonical poetry—Ovid's *Metamorphoses* XV.871 ff.; Horace's *Odes* III.xxx;

Shakespeare's *Sonnet* 55—in the claim it seems to make for a long shelf-life. But then brass is also 'brassy',—'impudently confident' says the dictionary, 'debased yet pretentious', or 'harsh and feelingless in tone'. And Prynne's poetry has been called all of these things by its detractors. (Brass is money too, muck-and-brass, and awareness of the 'material base' of human activity pervades this poetry, as we shall see in *Red D Gypsum*.)

But a 'through-composed' sequence offered as a single work is different again to a collection of discrete poems marshalled together under one title, and this has been 'late' Prynne's preferred mode. As successive 'collected' editions have appeared, the completely deliberated nature of his writing becomes clear: hardly any revisions are made, no works are dropped (apart from the anomalous first book), the sequence is not shuffled, each work from *Kitchen Poems* (1968) onwards is reproduced in precisely the same text. It is as if the occasion of the composition and setting down of the poem is utterly specific, the form and content are irrevocably cast in the moment of the writing, and to revise or attempt to partially rethink the composition would be a betrayal of the poem's originating integrity, when form inseparably became content. This too is unusual; other poets can be much more fidgety with their work, more open to the processes of revision. Robert Graves' *Collected* editions, for example, show a writer who continuously shuffled, suppressed, and re-organized his work throughout a lifetime.

If we are to think of Prynne's poetry as 'counter versed' (2.7), set quite deliberately against the conventional expectations for lyric poetry today, then we must accept that it calls for kinds of reading and attention not demanded by our most widely celebrated poets, such as Seamus Heaney, Carol Ann Duffy, or Liz Lochhead. This has obvious consequences for the scale and kind of his readership. Prynne has also, apparently quite deliberately, restricted his 'means of production and dissemination' to what is called 'small press' publication—again a characteristic of the 'new' poetry that developed from the late 1960s—avoiding or indeed rejecting the opportunity of publication by more conventionally established publishers and secure means of distribution. The *Poems* of 1998 was effectively the first 'mainstream' appearance for his work. Nor has Prynne followed the conventional way of 'being in the world' as a practising poet: he has given hardly any public readings of his work, taken no residencies, made no festival appearances, he maintains no personal website, and never enters for competitive prizes: certainly no interviews with Melvin Bragg. What are we to make of this?

For all his singularity, Prynne has always written within a supportive context of other poets and artists, British, European and American, all intent on 'making it new' (the war cry of the American Modernist Ezra Pound (1885–1972), committed to 'modernizing' poetry in English, and a key influence for Prynne). In that sense Prynne's career has been a collaborative project, drawing on a wide range of contemporary practices in writing and the culture of his time (see Further Reading for some of Prynne's contemporaries and associates engaged in similar kinds of experiment). As a way of coming to terms with these fundamental qualities and challenges of Prynne's poetry, let's describe some obvious features of the work. None of the later sequences offers a coherent, speaking persona, either clearly fictional, as in a dramatic monologue by Browning, for example, or a voice that can be confidently identified with what we know of the character and biography of the poet, as in the great Romantic 'conversation' poems such as Wordsworth's 'Lines Written above Tintern Abbey' or Coleridge's 'Frost at Midnight'. These models of a singular, observing poetic figure, tied into history and landscape by countless filiations, were real presences in Prynne's earlier work, notably *The White Stones* (1969), more problematically in all of his poetry after *Brass* (1971)— see, most recently, his 134-page critical commentary, *Field Notes: 'The Solitary Reaper' and Others* (2007). Refusing the figure of a persona with whom the reader might identify, or locate meanings within, was one of the most obvious challenges posed by Prynne's new 'poetic', or writing strategy—there are disconcertingly few pronouns, for example, in *Red D Gypsum* (Wilkinson 2006: 202).

This refusal of a persona was in part a rejection of 'confessional' poetry, and of poems that were predicated on particular experiences where the reader might identify straightforwardly with what the poem narrated, celebrated or lamented. It was very much a rejection of 'personality' from the reading-experience—not John Berryman, Robert Lowell, Sylvia Plath or Ted Hughes. The personal dimension of writing and performance is such an obvious appeal for most readers of poetry and for audiences at poetry readings, but it is not one that is offered by Prynne's writing. One way of viewing this is to think of much older kinds of poetic convention where the anonymity of the 'makar' was routine, as in ballads, epics, praise poems from warrior societies, or even devotional verse, all of which called on larger collectivities and belief systems than the mere personality of the poet. Works of the last few years that have enjoyed great success and large readerships, such as Ted Hughes' *Birthday Letters* (1998), which was manifestly written out of searing biographical experience, could not be further from Prynne's mode of writing, and the kind of reading that it requires. The poet described something like this stance in the following terms: 'It has mostly been my own aspiration, for example, to establish relations not personally with the reader, but with the world and its layers of shifted but recognisable usage; and thereby with the reader's own position within this world' (quoted in Dorward 2004). However, this poet is ever a tricksy spirit: one of Prynne's rare traces on the worldwideweb as a performer can be found under his name at http://archiveofthenow.com where he reads John Wieners' poem 'Cocaine': click and listen, and consider of his performance sounds like the poet I am describing.

If these poems do not offer us a coherent persona, nor do we find a coherent narrative, locale or time. In other words, Prynne's poetry since the early 1970s has challenged the reader to produce what linguistics terms 'cohesion', that is, a systematically accumulated meaning constructed from the myriad details of a text. We are offered arrays of language, drawing on a wide range of diction, specialisms and knowledge-bases, but there do not appear, for example, to be consistent image-clusters that can be confidently assembled as the reader proceeds through the sequence. And yet . . . there is an absolutely distinctive tone and texture to this poetry, with which any reader who persists will quickly become familiar, and in that sense there most definitely is a 'voice', but a 'text-voice' rather than a personality. And as you read to and fro in sequences such as *Red D Gypsum* you also begin to recognise a terrain, occasionally a landscape, certainly a complex locale, which has many simultaneous dimensions: a wood, an exploited landscape, cultivated fields, mines, rooms of several kinds—

trading rooms, for example, sites of violence, perhaps even of massacre . . . And there are 'internal' spaces too,—within bodies, explored as they are wounded and healed, certainly many different kinds of mental landscape, even the interiors of plant cells as they photosynthesize. Above all, entering the 'selvage obscure' (4.5) of *Red D Gypsum* we are within language-depths, at the switching points of thousands of words and phrases as 'we' the readers operate the language system, play the language game, or, as it simultaneously plays us. This is an extraordinary effect of Prynne's poetry when it is 'working' for a reader, and one that has become identified as central to his writing: the poems describe not so much a world, or people, or events as discrete, separate experiences, but rather the ways in which our consciousness *as* language constructs meaning, receives the world. In this sense, to read these texts for 'cohesion' in conventional terms is also mistaken: their poetic endlessly qualifies any resolved position—semantic, ethical, political, 'existential'—that the reader might be tempted to take, an infinitely provoking engagement.

After all these forbidding qualities, let's also be clear that there is a specific kind of music, of poetic beauty, to Prynne's lyricism, a strangeness made out of all kinds of diction. His poetry is at one with the long tradition of poets who suddenly make creative claim for utterly new kinds of language and thought which had previously been excluded from the narrow room of the lyric: Donne, *Lyrical Ballads*, T. S. Eliot. (Or does this writing so transgress literary conventions that it is pointless to continue thinking of it as 'lyric' at all? See Simon Perril 2003.) As with these distinguished predecessors, the words that Prynne's poems can enliven don't have to be rare or abstruse, because even the most apparently commonplace material can suddenly become complex, and take on a new, bright meaning and therefore interest. This is what good poetry can always do, which is to refresh our sense of the language. The title of *Red D Gypsum* has precisely this kind of interest. The pamphlet presents a capital D reversed-out in white on a blood-scarlet square, a 'sigil' or seal, according to Nolan. It looks for all the world like a convincingly commercial logo for an actual product. If you've been around DIY stores or builders' yards you might have come across Blue Circle Cement, so why not a Red D Gypsum? But then, who would want to read a poem about a bag of plaster?

2: A Brief Historie of Plaster

Gypsum in fact is a wonderful mineral, and one that has been used as a material and commodity throughout human history in myriad ways. The mineral exists in radically different forms; the fine-grained variety is known as alabaster, a soft, often translucent stone that has been beautifully carved and polished for millennia. Alabaster is generally pale in colour, but the stone can take on subtle tints, from fawns through to ochres and russets. A highly sophisticated school of alabaster sculptors flourished around Nottingham in the medieval period, carving intensely devotional statuary. As 'satin spar' gypsum is fibrous and sometimes opalescent, and in this form is used in jewellery. Ground down as crude gypsum, the sulphate takes on its most practical aspect when it is added to agricultural fertilizers, paper and textile production, plaster board and construction blocks—*The White Stones* become pulverized. Plaster of paris is used in schools, studios, and Accident and Emergency wards. This admirable mineral is a prime candidate for Prynne's poetic attention precisely because it is so inwoven with human activities across millennia.

A central reference work for reading Prynne's poetry is the most complete version of the *Oxford English Dictionary* that you can find. A good Reference Library will have the complete edition, in twenty-two volumes, or even offer access to the online version of the *Dictionary*, which is constantly updated. The *OED* is one of the great books of the world because it set new standards of accuracy and scope in recording not just current usage of words, but also their evolving history for as long as written records have been available; the latest edition also draws on a 'corpus' of spoken and recorded usage. This is a central concern of Prynne's poetry, and also for his 'day job' as a scholar and teacher of English literature. In a lecture, *Stars, Tigers and the Shape of Words* (1993), Prynne dwelt on this 'diachronic' aspect of language, that is, the study of language change over extended periods, describing it as 'an aggregating and proliferative instigation, recursively back-folding and cross-linking, and this kind of incorporative opportunism is idiomatic for a whole pattern of cultural practice in which language is a centrally-mediating agency' (34: quoted Basu 31). This actually sounds like a rather good description of Prynne's way of writing, an 'incorporative opportunism' and 'proliferative instigation'. The endless weave of reading *Red D Gypsum* certainly requires recursive 'back-folding and cross-linking' ('link' is a recurrent word in the poem). The entry for gypsum in the *OED* is in fact quite brief, but suggests how important the substance has been over time. The English word derives, without much modification, from the Latin and ultimately Greek words for chalk, in terms of chemical composition, 'Hydrous calcium sulphate, the mineral from which plaster of Paris is made'. And sure enough, the first reference, from as early as 1387, is to the large gypsum quarries outside Paris. A reference from 1662 refers to 'figures' or carvings made out of gypsum, and from the early nineteenth century to the agricultural use of gypsum as a field dressing or fertiliser ('Leaf paris green strikes a vein . . . run over in winded plaster cuts'—10.1 and 3).

A fascinating example of how gypsum may have affected human culture occurs in the North Yorkshire landscape around Thornborough. Here large caches of gypsum have over millennia dissolved through the action of underground streams and eventually washed away, with spectacular results at the land surface. Suddenly a deep, sometimes cavernous depression opens up as the soil mantle collapses into the void below, leaving a dramatically pitted terrain. During the later Neolithic period, perhaps responding to these mysterious depths that suddenly appeared, and which might even have taken lives, the local culture created a remarkable line of earthworks with a very particular orientation to the night sky. The three huge circles appear to mimic quite precisely the stars in the constellation of Orion that form the 'belt', in a (not quite) straight line. The outer banks of the circles were then plastered with wet gypsum which would have dried to a hard, high white, and the Yorkshire circles in 3000 BCE would have shone as brightly as the three great pyramids at Ghiza (which also, as it happens, echo the line of Orion's belt). This white 'dressing' of the ubiquitous Neolithic and early Bronze age henge monuments seems to have been widespread, found also, for example, at Avebury in Wiltshire. So Prynne has chosen a commonplace mineral that has been valued throughout human history. Thornborough isn't overtly present in *Red D Gypsum*, I think, but this kind of totemic value and cultural association is, at several levels of the poem.

3: 'raised D flash/on its matt red square' (11.3–4)

We can take the cover logo of *Red D Gypsum* as a way to begin reading the work. Is there an occulted meaning, a hidden clue in the 'Red D'? If there was a single, private signification to be discovered, like a child's puzzle book, let's say that would be a mean, ungenerous poetic strategy, 'private meanings' in the bad sense. Poetic meanings should be public, and multiple, there for the reader to infer and construct, your guess as good as mine, until we come to fit them to a larger account of the whole poem. And then the readings that seem most congruent, which contribute most to interpretation, will be the most effective. Words conjure other words, in so many ways; 'Red D' might suggest 'ready', apt for use, which the hero-mineral certainly is. Or is D a cipher-letter for another word . . . Danger, Death? Kevin Nolan suggests that Nathaniel Hawthorne's novel of persecution in Puritan New England, *The Scarlet Letter* (1850) haunts *Pearls That Were*, Prynne's sequence preceding *Red D Gypsum*. The heroine, Hester Prynne (make of that what you will), accused of adultery, is made to appear before her community wearing, as a badge of her shame, "in fine red cloth, surrounded with an elaborate embroidery and fantastic flourishes of gold thread . . . the letter A" (Hawthorne 1983: 163). Nolan also cites Poe's *The Masque of the Red Death* (1842), in which "Darkness and Decay and the Red Death held illimitable dominion over all" as one of the texts 'in play' for *Red D Gypsum* (Nolan 2003: 41). Nolan's reading of the sequence is a chilling one: "It is, perhaps, the most unsparing demonstration of Prynne's constant suspicion that poetry, like Prospero's castle, has been little more than an ego-fortress shielding the arbitrary whims of an icy, autocratic decisionism" (41). It's undeniable that 'Red' as a colour and meaning runs through the stanzas of the poem, for example, "its/divisible burden of stab-rufous scale" (2.3/4), perhaps a wounding; "Trailing up for/darker wads over red you said fast", (7.5–6) perhaps wound treatment. And red appears in different shades, as "Maroon pyrite" (8.3) or "massive indigo" (11.2), recalling the beautiful stainings found in the alabaster and satin spar forms of gypsum. The phrase in the text "raised D flash/on its matt red square" (11.3–4) might call up Red Square, Moscow, or the defensive squares assumed by British 'redcoat' infantry in eighteenth-

and nineteenth-century conflicts. And "the red and the white" was a well-established metonymy in ballad and lyric forms for 'the flesh', itself metonymic of desire, frailty, death.

Or are these just arbitrary associations such as any reader might happen to think of in relation to the phrase? In the only other extensive discussion of the poem to date, Jay Basu looks even more closely at the title word "Red", and finds that it might have been the earlier Latin form of the prefix 're-'. Basu then points out that this prefix seems to haunt the poem, appearing more than forty times, as well as embedding itself in other key words, 'three', 'trek' and so on. Basu cites definitions of this founding prefix as "(1) the opposition of an action; 'to fight against, resist'; (2) the reversal of an action, which may connote 'to unweave, unravel', or 'to uncover, lay bare'. All of these implications are at play in Prynne's text. There are multiple references . . . to resisted movement and violent obstruction" (Basu 2001: 27).

So much for the cover. (A thought—does the poem lose a vital dimension when it is reproduced, as in *Poems* (2005), without the careful format and logo of the original pamphlet? Many of Prynne's collections as first published, issued in a few hundred copies, are strikingly designed, the physical aspect of the cover and type seeming to inform the poems: this is powerfully true of *Brass*, *High Pink on Chrome*, *Word Order* and *Pearls That Were*. This aesthetic dimension of the text-as-volume is a direct consequence of their small-scale means of production, and cannot carry over into the more anonymous formats of wide-scale circulation.)

We then meet an epigraph, again a recurrent feature of Prynne's sequences, and defined by the trusty *OED* as, "A short quotation or pithy sentence placed at the commencement of a work . . . to indicate the leading idea or sentiment". Epigraphs can be weighty or teasing, the 'motto' of the text that they precede. Prynne's are often 'delphic', strange remarks that might have come from Apollo's oracle. A particularly enjoyable example is the epigraph to his 1997 sequence, *For the Monogram*, which is a quotation from the seventeenth-century philosopher Leibniz: "Why should the dog ever be displeased *spontaneously*?" Just how this squares with the text that follows is another question. *Red D Gypsum*'s epigraph is playful in a different way, and certainly Delphic: "The volatility smile is not symmetrical."—Lillian Chew.' Any ideas?

4: 'Options "smile" at traders, but that smile is not a source of happiness.' (Chance 2004)

When all else fails, google it, and we find a vast literature on a fascinating problem in world financial markets. On 'Black Monday', 19 October 1987, financial markets across the world fell by an unprecedented 23 per cent in a single day. This was probably caused by systemic failures in trading systems, chiefly the newly installed method of 'program trading', or computer-initiated buying and selling. Nothing like this had happened since the cataclysmic Wall Street Crash of 1929, which precipitated a decade of worldwide economic 'Depression'. During the faltering market recovery in the late 1980s some traders began to notice a disturbing new effect in the financial models which they used to calculate risk-and-return on traded stock. The volatility, or rate of price change for options on stock, had become much more difficult to predict: "the volatility surface of index options had become skewed" (Derman 2003). When plotted as a graph, the implied volatility for stocks over any given time appeared u-shaped, and this prompted the new phrase, "volatility smile". Conditions changed again: 'In more recent years the smile has mostly disappeared, and the relationship has sometimes been referred to as a skew or even a smirk' (Chance 2004).

By the early 1990s, following the collapse of the Soviet Union and the opening of new, worldwide market opportunities, "clients were much more interested in easy global investing, and [equity] derivatives provided some of the best methods" (Derman 2003), but the new, disturbing variable made it much more difficult to predict degrees of risk. In October 2008 the volatility smile morphed into a snarl when a catastrophic market failure brought the entire world's financial system perilously close to total collapse, with unimaginable consequences for us all. A sum equivalent to one sixth of global GDP has been committed to sustain the banking and financial sectors, with no clear guarantee that even this will be sufficient. It's a small consolation, but perhaps these appalling developments make *Red D Gypsum* even more readable, truly a text for the times.

As with the utile commodity, gypsum, Prynne's epigraph to the sequence calls up many dimensions: how are the world financial markets managed? What consequences flow from the new unpredictability? This concern with fundamental aspects of resource and finance haunts Prynne's collections, beginning with the unpromising title of *Kitchen Poems* in 1968. The cover of the original pamphlet graphed the exploitation of the North Sea for natural gas extraction, and this brassily declared a new kind of poetry with some very up-to-the-minute concerns. *Down Where Changed* (1979) was a puzzling title when it first appeared, on a somber brown cover to what is a pretty glum sequence: it almost certainly implied that 'the market' is down, where changed. We can therefore hope to track financial dealing and option-taking through the text defiles of *Red D Gypsum*.

5: 'a hedged future' (20.7)

We've established some possible ranges of meaning for the title and epigraph of *Red D Gypsum*: what is it like to read the verses? Let's see what might be set racing in the first stanza:

> Now trek inter-plate reversion to earth buy out
> as waters buried or get carrier up ready put
> across gypsum branch effaced, as root planed
> for don't now look to demand new birds in talent
> from turf stripped to fibre. Rip brace out here
> on the fringe reckless bestowing taint by the mart
> chosen, tamper nickel token lunge to bite you may
> cover down over, a flawless glucose shimmered sky.

We are "trekking" into many different terrains, above all that of language-in-history, a journey that could take us anywhere. We are moving among many different kinds of "plate", or surface, and the extraction and exploitation of many kinds of resource is under way. There is bargaining and exchange at work, violent processes incurring damage; there seems to be counterfeiting of coinage, "tampering", which can be tested by "biting" the coin, the "nickel token". Investments are traded and potential losses are perhaps covered, and at the end of the stanza there is "a flawless glucose shimmered sky." This description already fails to cover the multitude of options that the lines offer, because it ignores so many details. The grammar of the sequence elides phrases and clauses so that it is impossible to finally resolve options on meaning. At the end of the first line 'buy out' ought to function as a verb, according to the *Oxford Dictionary for Writers and Editors*, since it is written as two words, but the grammar of the line encourages me at least to read as it as a noun phrase, an 'earth buyout', which would be to possess a controlling share of the world.

And then how does the second line qualify what we take from the first? Who or what is the "carrier"? In the third line is the "branch" a vein of gypsum, or is it the 'branch' of a company, or is it also to be associated with 'root', as in 'root and branch', a phrase meaning 'fundamental', 'all-encompassing', for example 'root and branch reform', but here more likely destruction, since it is 'effaced' and 'planed for', as if in some radical extractive process. And who or what are these 'new birds', are they really "talent", desirable, or does it mean they are part of an account ('talent' is one of the oldest words in English meaning 'money' or 'value'), or that they are talented, have ability? And then, as a profound grammatical relief, the stanza resolves with a descriptive phrase, lovely in its way, but still enigmatic, that "flawless glucose shimmered sky". Yet here too options are kept open; if "glucose shimmered" describes a sky, it ought to be hyphenated; since it isn't, "shimmered" could be a verb . . . but then how could "sky" be its object? (This line also seems to develop the epigraph to *Word Order* (1989), "*Strew sugar over the zephyrs*"; here is an eye for candied skies.)

Let's assume that this first stanza heads up the poem in the sense of setting an agenda, starting at least some of the hares that will run through the entire sequence. (In fact, it can't be quite as simple as this, because the second stanza seems to flag up even more ranges of option-taking and option-trading.) "Plates" (1.1) recur through the poem, as working spaces, malleable surfaces, electrostatic zones; "inter-plate reversion" (1.1); "zinc plates" (3.5); "Tonic D plate" (28.4); "Red plate to red/snapper filament" (28.6–7). The trek is certainly sustained, often through woods, traditionally the place in which to become lost; in the Middle Ages a wood was allegorically the world of mere matter that betrayed or destroyed higher aspirations. Prynne puns on European literature's most famous allegorical wood, Dante's *selva oscura*—dark wood—in which the persona loses his way at the beginning of the *Divine Comedy*. In *Red D Gypsum* this becomes "underside selvage obscure" (4.5), though "selvage" is also "over-determined" (that is, has more senses) as a tract or margin of land, or else the edge of a length of material, or even the layer around a metallic vein in mining—this journey is through a complex series of language margins, not just a wood.

At about mid-way the trek seems to have reached a critical point, "On the march." This is a strangely elegiac verse, full sentences re-emerge, offering hints of tragic event:

> Simmer down your almost last arrivals
> rendered like lard, leaf from stem reversion. Will she
> finger the flute, cold and wet, breathing on through it
> but making no fit sound . . . take the folded
> cloth in both hands, put it square on, notice a ring
> just touching against the horizon and emptied out flat.
>
> (14.1–4, 6–8)

(But, again, I have 'naturalized' the verse by omitting lines and phrases that don't square with this realist reading. (For 'Bad Naturalization' and an early reading of Prynne, see Forrest-Thomson (1978).) The central verse seems to narrate a violent, rapacious hunt, "The bark running with sperm, fierce fox-cry repeated,/now receding across a trail of scouring must." (15.1–2) The illusion of a recoverable narrative is decisively dissolved with the next stanza, which has some of the most impacted, compacted lines where plant physiology and photosynthetic processes emerge, "Flow/flow my phloem dear ones, fibre life thickens limpid" (18.2–3). Sometimes you feel as if you are in the midst of a four-dimensional crossword, with the most cryptic clues demanding an answer: "Greeting announcers/touch up the fender hardly, poorly provided in benison" (12.7–8). Are these hypermarket 'greeters', talking up trade in the parking lot, but giving no genuine welcome at all?

The sense of an encrypted narrative returns at stanza 19:

> They were astute and dumb, voiceless fixed next to the
> platinum link; cast-off on impulse . . .

> In full view of the reaction process they were instructed
> to say nothing, which with one accord truly they did.
>
> (19.1–2, 7–8)

What is being witnessed, by whom? Is this a guilty complicity, and who is calling for it? Threesomes haunt the narrative throughout, "Three trammel birds", (5.1), a "trio" (6.4), "all three enter now" (9.7), "Three on deck" (11.7), "two rising, limit to three" (22.5). Kevin Nolan gives a philosophical gloss here: "The warning signs in *Red D Gypsum* alert poet and reader alike that the 'lyric interior' is not a redoubt, or vantage, from which the all consuming Other can be viewed. Rather, Prynne appears to suggest that the experience of self-negation demands the relocation of subjectivity in a third space beyond the reflexive dyad of self and other" (Nolan 2003: 43).

At stanza 25, we seem to be witnessing some kind of terra-forming process, nature 'naturing' through massive geological events:

> . . . Snake roots break their chain
> in fighting harvest, pushing up, hillsides arch and worry
> off their rug, in clouds of gonad dust. They got seed
> broken, close on breeding uproar, now dark shades clatter
> force them down to simmer under foot. Thirst replays
> triple throated scan for gaps, entry and pallet flicks
> deeper going down, root burning. Bribing their locks.
>
> (25.2–8)

This passage may have some relation to the lovely section in Milton's *Paradise Lost*, Book Seven, where the Archangel Raphael recounts God's creation of all things out of Chaos:

> Immediately the Mountains huge appear
> Emergent, and their broad bare back up heave
> Into the Clouds . . .
> The grassie Clods now calv'd, now half appear'd
> The tawny Lyon, pawing to get free
> His hinder parts, then springs as broke from Bonds
> And Rampant shakes his brinded Mane . . .
>
> (VII.285–7, 463–6)

And is there some kind of descent to the shades of Avernus, past a triple-headed Cerberus? Milton does perhaps haunt the text here; the next stanza seems to describe a kind of Fall,

> Flaw on the ground too many grappled fruiting body
> assets quilted there, echoes of milky cash-in plushy
> arrived for grand style averted, do it.
>
>   (26.1–3)

And cultivating an empty 'grand style' was precisely what Milton was criticized for by T. S. Eliot and F. R. Leavis, among others: 'in this Grand Style, the medium calls pervasively for a kind of attention, compels an attitude towards itself, that is incompatible with sharp, concrete realization' (Leavis *Revaluation*, 1936, quoted Ricks 1963: 3)

How do the risk-takers of the equity futures market figure in the poem? In the second stanza someone is "running a hot risk counter versed bid up" (2.7); in stanza thirteen "blue sky chancers want/ to peer out on offer" (13.3–4); there's definitely trading in stanza nineteen, "Bark to excited flood/in facile ketone derivatives will instigate regraded/bond preening: wound up and down on a glassy slide." (19.4–6). But looking hard down a microscope may not be of help. "In full view of the reaction process they were instructed/to say nothing. Which with one accord truly they did." (19.7–8) Traders bound to the secrets of the market? Scientists witnessing a new dangerous procedure? In the next stanza, the market seems to be in play: "Without/fuss or thickness playing over a hedged future, links/ make a tight bumpy ride duly sliced up on account." (20.6–8). 'Hedge funds' are financial devices only available to wealthy individuals and institutions, and which deploy the most aggressive kinds of strategy in negotiating, buying and selling stocks. They are able to do this because they are (or were) not subject to the high degree of regulation that applies to the more secured, less venturesome 'mutual' funds, and as such, hedge funds have been deeply implicated in the near total market failure of October 2008. In stanza 26, after the Miltonic 'creation' moment, "tracker funding holds/its losses under grassy slopes preening the time of day" (26.7–8), a kind of strange mingling of financial engineering and pastoral landscape. The final market play seems to be in the penultimate stanza,

A Manner of Utterance

> Top-work the frame to chalk white yet against less
> clear tremolo flotation, sudden demerged racing
> downsize nutrient plume to risk appetite so born
> (29.1–3)

How does the sequence close? 'Bark' has recurred in this poem (with a nod, perhaps, to the *Barque* imprint) after the vivid moment in stanza fifteen, both as verb and noun; 'three-stanza barking magnified' (17.3), "Bark to excited flood" (19.4), "Newly/marine devices glimmer at a bark scripture advented" (21.4–7), "phantom bark entries" (23.7), and it figures in the final lines:

> . . .Vivid strips
> of tree bark circle the room its introit fading flood
> across broken sky reflexed, repelled threads mercuric
> took bounds remontant to grasp out along its line.
> (30.5–8)

The 're-' prefix recurs in the strangely heraldic "remontant", in fact a nineteenth-century botanical term for roses flowering twice within the season. As elsewhere in the poem, one word seems to engender another, since here the stanza began with "Surmounted"; it may be that the "silent witnesses" from stanza 19 also recur here, still "subrepted to mute", where 'subreption' may be 'the suppression of a truth or concealment of facts' for personal gain, or more abstractly, 'deceptive representation'.

6: 'vulpine night screaming out' (24.6)

Here is another reading of one of the 'late late' sequences that has hardly begun. I've tried to follow what a reader might take to be fundamental themes in the poem, from title, epigraph and imagery, but I've failed to make them cohere in any sustained way. For as many themes as I've picked, many more suggest themselves at each re-reading—a savage hunting, metamorphosis, modes of information display . . . By far the larger part of the sequence remains unreadable in the terms proposed. What kind of coherence and augmented meanings can we expect to find in such complex texts? There is so much to think about as you move from word to word and line to line in this poetry, working hard to construct larger, supra-segmental meaning, and the poem always escaping, always offering more, if it has intrigued you sufficiently, if you have found enough satisfaction in the effort of reading. There is no other poetry quite like this, though all interesting poetry works to some degree in these ways. And again, as with all worthwhile activity, what you learn reading Prynne can illuminate so much else. It's like listening to a very challenging twentieth-century composer such as Alban Berg or Anton von Webern, and then hearing all other music much more clearly, as if your ears have been cleaned out and your hearing re-tuned. 'The novel aspects of his style (melodic and harmonic fragmentation, wide intervallic leaps, unusual use of dissonance and timbres, ascetic sparseness of texture, and extreme conciseness of form) at first disconcerted those conditioned to the opulence of the late Romantic era' (*Britannica* 2003)—this description of Webern's style would seem to confirm Prynne's obligations to classical European Modernism. Reading one great or even good poem adjusts the way that you read thereafter. It might dissatisfy you with some kinds of reading, as no longer challenging enough, or even fraudulent—those books and authors that seem to offer more than they actually deliver when you think about them as intensely as the reading of Prynne calls for.

Reading this kind of text engages us in a process that always promises new links, sudden connections, but which never delivers the finality of a single closure, a finale that resolves all. The poetry keeps beguiling us through fascinating defiles of meaning and word-history, which is necessarily our history too, however remote-seeming, but also through the lyricism of the writing, the loveliness—more often, the 'estrangedness' (look it up in *OED*!), of words and phrases. Our affective responses to language and meaning, those drawing on our emotions, are crucially involved with this reading, and it would be a complete error to dismiss poetry such as this as merely 'academic'— writing that simply plays heartless intellectual games. Ideas are passions too. Reading this poetry can be as exciting as flying through landscapes of information and meaning: William Gibson's *Neuromancer* (1984) is a kind of metaphor for this process, navigating data banks of compelling materials as if your life depended on it. This poetry certainly takes you to some great corners of the dictionary, and so necessarily, of language-history: 'ataraxy', 'the condition of a quiet and settled life', (Florio's *Montaigne*, 1603), and which this poetry does not bestow.

Perhaps this is a reading-experience—and perhaps also a writing-experience—quite like James Joyce's last great experiment-novel, *Finnegans Wake*, which, Joyce claimed, was not written by himself but by "you, and you, and you, and that man over there and that girl at the next table". By which he meant that he was hoping to create an ur-language in the novel that could be common to us all. But Prynne's poetic surely doesn't possess that kind of benign universality. The ways in which we read these poems are the strategies that we have to develop to move through language; they are also the ways in which language acquires us, in the sense that the word hoard bestows so many options for meanings, a virtually infinite array of possible connectivities within which we play, as if in a game.

What might it be like to write this kind of work? How conscious might you have to be of all the possibilities?—Try it for yourself; several others poets are doing precisely that. It may be that parameters are set, a kind of agenda is constructed, but the way of the writing itself then offers possibilities that were beyond imagining. This is a not uncommon ambition among writers, to be able to invent 'beyond-oneself', when the writing becomes a half-conscious collaboration between the individual and the enabling resources of poetic conventions and language-history, that is, of culture. Think of those old 'makars' of epic and ballad and devotional writing. The writer him/herself may be as puzzled as their readers are by some of the further reaches of what they merely happened to write. Does this make such a poem fraudulent, or compelling? Now read and write on.

Further Reading

A comprehensive bibliography of Prynne's poetry and prose, together with a selection articles and reviews available online is compiled by Nate Dorward (2004) at http://www.pages.sprint.ca/ndorward/files/prynne.html

Prynne, J.H. (2005) *Poems*. Tarset: Bloodaxe Books. Contains all the uncollected poems, collections and sequences to 2004, excluding the first, suppressed book, *Force of Circumstance* (1962).

—(2007) *Field Notes: 'The Solitary Reaper' and Others*, Cambridge. Distributed by Barque Press, http://www.barquepress.com

Basu, Jay (2001) 'The Red Shift. Trekking J.H. Prynne's *Red D Gypsum*', *The Cambridge Quarterly*, 30/1, pp.19–36.

Chance, Don (2004) 'The Volatility Smile', *Financial Engineering News*. http://www.bus.lsu.edu/academics/finance/faculty/dchance/Vita. html

Clark, Steve (2003) 'Prynne and the Movement', *Jacket* 24, http://www. jacketmagazine.com/24/clark-s.html

Derman, Emanuel (2003) 'Laughter in the Dark—The Problem of the Volatility Smile', http://www.ederman.com/new/docs/euronext-volatility_smile.pdf

Duncan, Andrew (2003) 'Response to Steve Clark's "Prynne and the Movement"', *Jacket* 24, http://www.jacketmagazine.com/24/duncan. html

Forrest-Thomson, Veronica (1978) *Poetic Artifice. A Theory of Twentieth-Century Poetry*, Manchester University Press.

Hawthorne, Nathaniel (1850), *The Scarlet Letter. A Romance*. New York: The Library of America, Viking (1983).

Mengham, Rod, and John Kinsella (1999) 'An Introduction to the Poetry of J.H. Prynne', *Jacket* 7, http://www.jacket.zip.com.au/jacket07/ prynne-jk-rm.html

Nolan, Kevin (2003) 'Capital Calves: Undertaking an Overview', *Jacket* 24, http://www.jacketmagazine.com/24/nolan.html; and see Wilkinson (2006).

Perril, Simon (2003) 'Hanging on Your Every Word: J.H. Prynne's *Bands Around The Throat* and a Dialectics of Planned Impurity', *Jacket* 24, http://www.jacketmagazine.com/24/perril.html [Reprinted in this volume, pp.83–103]

Ricks, Christopher (1963) *Milton's Grand Style*, Oxford.

Wilkinson, John (2006), 'Tenter Ground', review of *Poems* (2005), *Notre Dame Review* 22, http://www.nd.edu/~ndr/issues/ndr22/John%20 Wilkinson/Wilkinson-review.pdf

Some associated or comparable poets:

John Ashbery (1972) *Three Poems*. New York: Viking Press. See Nigel Wheale, 'A New Subjectivity? John Ashbery's *Three Poems*' in *The Postmodern Arts*. London: Routledge, 1995.

Paul Celan (1980) *Poems. A Bilingual Edition, selected, translated and introduced by Michael Hamburger*. Manchester: Carcanet Press. One of the few poets actually named in Prynne's work, see 'Es Lebe der König' *(for Paul Celan, 1920–1970)'*, *Poems* p.169. As a Jew from Central Europe, Celan suffered more than his share of the time's horrors and tragedy. He became celebrated as the most original poetic voice of those experiences in German. See John Felstiner, *Paul Celan. Poet, Survivor, Jew*. New Haven: Yale University Press, 1995, and Anne Carson, *Economy of the Unlost. (Reading Simonides of Keos with Paul Celan)*. Princeton, NJ: Princeton University Press, 1999.

W. S. Graham (2004) *New Collected Poems* edited by Matthew Francis. London: Faber. A poet in some ways as individual as Prynne, and as rewardingly challenging, though from an earlier generation and a very different context.

R. F. Langley (2000) *Collected Poems*, Carcanet/*infernal methods*, for sequences that make interesting comparisons with Prynne's contemporaneous work.

Denise Riley (ed.) (1992) *Poets on Writing. Britain, 1970–1991*. London: Macmillan. A collection of essays including some of Prynne's interlocutors and poets influenced by him. Commentary on his work is almost exclusively by male poets and critics; is there anything to make of this?

Denise Riley (1993) *Mop Mop Georgette*. London: Reality Street Editions. A poet whose challenging manner and content is a rewarding contrast to Prynne's work. And see her *The Words of Selves. Identification, Solidarity, Irony*, Chapter Three, 'Lyric Selves'. Stanford: Stanford University Press, 2000.

Peter Riley (1995) *Alstonefield. Stanzas unfinished*. London/Plymouth: Oasis Books /Shearsman Books. Expanded edition: *Alstonefield: a poem*. Manchester: Carcanet Press, 2003. A precisely located sequence, rewardingly different again from either those of Langley or Prynne.

César Vallejo (2005) *Trilce*, edited and translated by Michael Smith and Valentino Gianuzzi. Exeter: Shearsman Books. This is a 'wild card', but Vallejo's *Trilce*, written in Peru in 1922, is another classic, baffling and beguiling poetic sequence that seemed to come from nowhere, in terms of its form and enigmatic content. *Trilce* therefore has the status of *The Waste Land* or *Ulysses* for Latin-American literature, and strangely, it was written in the year of publication of both those works—what *was* it about 1922?

A Various Art (1987) edited by Andrew Crozier and Tim Longville, Manchester: Carcanet Press, collects poets working around Prynne.

Contributors

Ian Brinton was formerly Head of English at Leeds Grammar School, Sevenoaks School and Dulwich College. He is Chair of the Secondary Schools' Committee for the English Association and edits *The Use of English*. He has published a book on *Great Expectations* and another, *Contemporary Poetry: Poets and Poetry Since 1990*, for the C.U.P. series, Contexts in Literature.

David Caddy edits the international literary magazine, *Tears in the Fence,* and presents *So Here We Are: Poetic Letters From England* on MiPoradio. His most recent poetry books are *The Willy Poems* (Clamp Down Press USA 2004) and *Man In Black* (Penned In The Margins 2007). He regularly reviews for *The Use of English*, the journal of the English Association, and the online journal, *Oranges & Sardines.*

Ian Friend is a British-born and Australian-resident visual artist. Recent solo shows include *Thirty Years of Works on Paper 1977–2007* (QUT Art Museum, Brisbane). His work is in public collections in both Australia and the U.K.

Richard Humphreys was a curator at Tate for many years as well as Head of Education and the organiser of many conferences and events. He was a founding member of the London Consortium, a collaborative PhD programme. He has written books and curated exhibitions on many subjects, including Ezra Pound and the visual arts, Kurt Schwitters, Wyndham Lewis, Futurism and British landscape art. He is currently writing a history of Sidney Sussex College, Cambridge.

Li Zhimin is Associate Professor at the School of Foreign Studies, Guangzhou University, and is Director of both its Foreign Languages Training Center and its Chinese and Western Cultural Study Institute. He is also a Fellow of the British and American Language and Literature Studies Institute of Sun Yat-sen University, and of the English Poetry Studies Institute (EPSI) at Sun Yat-sen University. He is Secretary-General of the English Poetry Studies Association of China, Director (Board Member) of Chinese / American Association for Poetry and Poetics (CAAP) and has been the prime mover of The Pearl River Poetry Conference, a gathering of Chinese and English poets held in Guangzhou in 2005 and 2008.

   Li Zhimin's publications reflect his broad interests in English and Chinese modernist and contemporary poetry and their interrelations, in pedagogy, and in poetic and translation theory. He is himself a poet and a translator of contemporary English poetry into Chinese, was a Fulbright Scholar at the University of California, Santa Barbara, in 2008.

Rod Mengham is Reader in Modern English Literature at the University of Cambridge, where he is also Curator of Works of Art at Jesus College. He is the author of books on Charles Dickens, Emily Brontë and Henry Green, as well as of *The Descent of Language* (1993). He has edited collections of essays on contemporary fiction, violence and avant-garde art, and the fiction of the 1940s. He is also the editor of the Equipage series of poetry pamphlets and co-editor and co-translator of *Altered State: the New Polish Poetry* (Arc Publications, 2003) and co-editor of *Vanishing Points: New Modernist Poems* (Salt, 2005). His own poems have been published under the title *Unsung: New and Selected Poems* (Folio/Salt, 1996; 2nd edition, 2001). His most recent books are *Thomas Hardy's Shorter Fiction*, co-written with Sophie Gilmartin (Edinburgh University Press, 2007) and *Parleys and Skirmishes* [poems] with photographs by Marc Atkins (Ars Cameralis, 2007).

Simon Perril teaches at De Montfort University, Leicester. His poetry collections include *Hearing is Itself Suddenly a Kind of Singing*, and the recently completed *Nitrate*. He has also edited *Tending the Vortex: the Works of Brian Catling* and the forthcoming *Salt Companion to John James*.

Keston Sutherland is a poet and a lecturer in English at the University of Sussex. He edits Barque Press and the journal *Quid*. His books include *Hot White Andy* and *Neocosis*. A full list of publications is available on his homepage at the University of Sussex.

John Douglas Templeton is a composer and librarian. He studied in London with Diana Burrell, in her prime, and he now lives in Glasgow.

Erik Ulman is currently a Lecturer in Music at Stanford University. He studied composition at the University of California, San Diego, working principally with Brian Ferneyhough, as well as with Helmut Lachenmann at the Stuttgart Musikhochschule on a DAAD grant. He has taught music at UCSD and the University of Illinois at Urbana-Champaign, and his music has been performed around the world by many leading soloists and ensembles. In December 2006 Ulman was awarded a commission from the Fromm Foundation at Harvard for *Canto XXV*, a cello and piano duo for Rohan de Saram. He was a composer-in-residence at Musiques Démesurées in Clermont-Ferrand in June 2007, and a resident artist at the Djerassi Program in Woodside in Summer 2008. Since 2004 Ulman and Marcia Scott have organized five Poto Festivals, a forum for artists in diverse media (potoweb.org).

Nigel Wheale's most recent poetry collection is *Raw Skies* (Shearsman, 2005).

Lightning Source UK Ltd.
Milton Keynes UK
30 October 2010

162160UK00001B/14/P

9 781848 610439